ETHNIC SURVIVAL IN AMERICA

Program in Judaic Studies
Brown University
BROWN STUDIES ON
JEWS AND THEIR SOCIETIES
Edited by
Jacob Neusner,
Wendell S. Dietrich, Ernest S. Frerichs,
Calvin Goldscheider, William Scott Green, Alan Zuckerman

Number 7
ETHNIC SURVIVAL IN AMERICA
An Ethnography of a Jewish Afternoon School

by
David Schoem

ETHNIC SURVIVAL IN AMERICA
An Ethnography of a Jewish Afternoon School

by
David Schoem

Scholars Press
Atlanta, Georgia

ETHNIC SURVIVAL IN AMERICA
An Ethnography of a Jewish Afternoon School

by
David Schoem

Copyright © 1989 Brown University

All rights reserved. No part of this work may be reproduced or transmitted in any form or by any means, electronic or mechanical, including photocopying and recording, or by means of any information storage or retrieval system, except as may be expressly permitted by the 1976 Copyright Act or in writing from Brown Judaic Studies, Brown University, Box 1826, Providence, RI 02912.

Library of Congress Cataloging-in-Publication Data
Schoem, David Louis.
  Ethnic survival in america : an ethnography of a Jewish afternoon school / by David Schoem.
    p. cm — (Brown studies on Jews and their societies : no. 7)
  Bibliography: p.
  ISBN 1-55540-265-8
    1. Jewish religious schools—United States—Case studies
  2. Jews—United States—Cultural assimilation—Case studies.
  3. Jews—United States—Identity—Case studies. I. Title
  II. Series
  BM109.C6S36   1988   89-4149
  305.8 '924'073—dc10   CIP
  ISBN 1-930675-17-8 (paper)

Printed in the United States of America
on acid-free paper

To Mom and Dad
Who Have Always Been My Very Finest Teachers

Contents

Acknowledgements ix

PART I
INTRODUCTION

1. The Jews and the Jewish School: Ethnic Minority-Majority Relations 3
2. Methodology 13

PART II
IDENTITY AND COMMUNITY

3. The Anti-Anti-Semites and the Non-Non-Jews 23
4. Searching for the Jewish Community 39

PART III
INSIDE THE JEWISH AFTERNOON SCHOOL

5. Arriving at Shalom School: Why Are We Here 53
6. Problematic Assumptions and Self-Deception 63
7. A Confusion of Purpose in the Classroom 81
8. One People, Many Conflicts 107
9. Success in the Short Term: Survival and Identification 121

PART IV
ETHNIC SURVIVAL AND ETHNIC AUTHENTICITY

10. Beyond Survival: Is There Hope for Substance and Authenticity 135
Notes 145
Bibliography 147

ACKNOWLEDGEMENTS

I am deeply indebted to the many people who have helped in the course of this study from its inception to its present form.

John U. Ogbu, Sheila S. Walker, John U. Michaelis, and Ronald G. Wolfson offered critical insight and constant encouragement throughout several drafts of the book. Their support, dedication, and unrelenting demand for excellence has been deeply appreciated.

I am thankful to the Dushkin Prize for Jewish Education from the Institute for Contemporary Jewry of the Hebrew University of Jerusalem and also to the Program on Conflict Management Alternatives of The University of Michigan for their support towards this publication and my research.

My colleagues from the Conference on Research on Jewish Education in Jerusalem and the CAJE Research Network on Jewish Education have served as a sustaining source of support and learning. Harold Himmelfarb, Arnold Dashefsky, Barry Chazan, and Hyman Pomerantz have offered critical feedback and valuable guidance. Along the way, Walter Ackerman, Harlene Appleman, Isa Aron, Adrienne Bank, Sheldon Dorph, Seymour Fromer, Abraham Gannes, Joel Grishaver, Barry Holtz, Leora Isaacs, Stuart Kelman, Joseph Lukinsky, Judah Pilch, Edy Rauch, Bernard Reisman, Ron Reynolds, Michael Zeldin, and Walter Zenner have shared insights, encouragement and friendship. Thanks also to Susan Gold, Eileen Kane, and Doris Walker for their personal and technical support.

My most important thanks goes to my own Jewish family, to Karyn, my wife, and to Adina and Shana, my daughters, for their love and encouragement, insight and understanding, laughter and smiles.

And you shall teach them to your children, and you shall speak of them when you stay at home, and when you go on your way, and when you lie down, and when you rise up.

(Deuteronomy VI:7)

I guess if there weren't so many pressures and directions—what with work and bills and taxes and weeds—we might sit down with books and read about Judaism. But hell, we'd rather watch the Super Bowl.

(Ed Finklestein, parent at Shalom School)

PART I
INTRODUCTION

Chapter One

THE JEWS AND THE JEWISH SCHOOL: ETHNIC MINORITY—MAJORITY RELATIONS

This is a study of the Jewish people within one suburban community in America. Looking at this particular ethnic group, the Jews, and at one of its institutions, the Jewish supplementary school, this study examines the conflicts and dilemmas that this ethnic group faces in its effort to survive and in its attempt to maintain a substantive and authentic identity.

The study explores people's lives, thoughts, and perceptions of what it means to be Jewish in suburban America. It studies what happens in the Jewish school and explores the purpose and value of the school in terms of the broader issues of Jewish survival and Jewish authenticity in a pluralistic society. The study examines the relationship between what is taught in the Jewish school and how the Jewish people connected with the school live and perceive the way they live in America.

Like other ethnic groups that are culturally subordinate, the Jewish people face the problem of maintaining and transmitting their cultural authenticity—even their very survival as an ethnic group—while living in a society whose dominant culture is different. At one extreme, some argue (Sowell 1981) that the Jews are the model ethnic group, the ethnic American success story. According to this argument, not only have Jews achieved success in secular education, in upward socio-economic mobility, and in political influence in the United States, but they have also achieved a nearly unprecedented level of renewal and strength in Jewish study, organization, and communal activity (Silberman 1985).

Others worry about just the opposite, that the Jews are in danger of disappearance either through assimilation, intermarriage, internal division, etc. (Cohen 1987). Goldscheider (1986, 1984) argues that the Jewish community today is powerful and cohesive and that the Jews are in a period of transformation. Cohen (1988) effectively poses that "transformationist" view against a more pessimistic outlook, what he calls the "assimilationist" view, which worries for the very survival of the Jews.

The findings of this study and, indeed, the dominant and sustaining view of Jewish life in this regard for the past thirty years has been the recognition of a loss of substance and authenticity in Jewish life and Jewish identity yet not to a point that threatens Jewish survival. This view stands in contrast to both the transformationist/renewal view and the assimilationist/disappearance view. The Jews have found themselves unable to participate fully in both their own and the dominant culture. They have found themselves caught between their "idealized identity"—Jewish values, and their "pragmatic instrumental preference"—secular rewards and values (Spindler 1976; Schoem 1982).

Scholars and researchers of American Jewish life have used a variety of labels to describe this non-substantive identity, such as "apathetic identification" (Cahnman 1955), "symbolic Judaism" (Gans 1956), "inauthentic Jew" (Sartre 1965), "marginal Judaism" (Sklare 1967) and "false consciousness" (Rosenthal 1970). Glazer observed in 1954 that "From the point of view of any classic or legitimate idea of "nation," the nations of Poles, Jews, Italians, and so on, that now and then show themselves in American politics and culture, are empty or ghost nations." More recently, DeVos (1975) has commented on this subject saying, "Already some individuals who consider themselves Jews have no remaining special linguistic heritage; they no longer adhere to any of the beliefs of Judaism nor to any customs peculiar to Jewish culture, and they do not believe that Jews comprise any special or distinct racial group. How, then, can they continue to feel that being Jewish is of importance in their sense of social self, or ethnic identity?"

These different readings of the Jewish place in American society point out the complex framework of contacts and relations between Jews and the majority non-Jewish society. Certainly throughout American history there has been a constant tension in maintaining the unity of one America with the presence of many different groups. The traditional view has been that of an America that has welcomed people of diverse backgrounds with open arms. However, others have argued (Steinberg 1981) that such a view represents more myth than reality and is actually contrary to the experience of many or even most ethnic groups in the United States. That continuing tension of ethnic minority-majority relations, in particular the tension between Americanization and cultural pluralism, and also the possible limits within cultural pluralism itself, serve as the context for this study.

The Jews of this community (to be known as Apple River) and this school (to be known as Shalom School), who will be described in the pages to follow, are neither in danger of assimilation to the point of not surviving, nor are they part of a transformation or renewal of the Jews (Cohen 1988; Goldscheider 1986). Surely the survival of the Jewish people will continue to be an ongoing concern for the Jews and certainly there may be pockets of Jewish renewal that lend support to Silberman's (1985) optimistic perspective, but the rich qualitative data of this study help to give a more in-depth and clearer understanding of the statistical data that have led to the transformationist-assimilationist conceptions. This research demonstrates that the people of this community are Americans who happen to be Jewish and who struggle with great confusion and little success trying to find meaning in their lives as Jews. Their story reveals the lack of substance to their Jewish identity and Jewish living, and the loss of meaning that being Jewish holds for them in their daily lives.

It informs both Jews and other ethnic minority communities that when there is a very high degree of both cultural and socio-economic integration, there may be limits to cultural pluralism in the struggle for ethnic substance, meaning, and authenticity.

The Jews and Ethnic Minority-Majority Conflict

Definitions: The Jews as an Ethnic Group

The definition of an ethnic group that is used in this study draws from the work of many in the field, including DeVos (1975), Parsons (1975), Kallen (1956), Gordon (1964) and Isajiw (1974). However, the changing characteristics of one ethnic group relative to other ethnic groups and cultures in the society make it difficult to develop a definition that is entirely precise, explicit, and without qualification. With that caution in mind, the definition used in this study is as follows: An ethnic group is a self-perceived group of people who are transgenerational, who share a common sense of peoplehood, and who hold common historical roots, a common sense of historical continuity, and a common culture that includes a common set of traditions. This common culture may include in whole or in part aspects such as religion, language, and geography. In addition, the group may have shared genetic characteristics. Inclusion in the group is most commonly involuntary. As a qualification of this definition, it should be understood that at any given time various aspects of the common culture and traditions, and the common sense of historical continuity may neither be shared nor practiced in all respects by all members of the group.

The Jewish people fit this definition along with the accompanying statement of qualification. The Jews are both a self-perceived group and perceived by others as a group, are transgenerational, and hold common historical roots, a common sense of historical continuity and a common culture that includes common traditions. They have a religion which is Judaism, a language which is Hebrew, and a geographical center which is Israel. Inclusion in the Jewish group is usually by circumstance of birth although conversion is possible. There are also certain genetic disorders that are generally limited to Jewish people. Finally, and as a qualification to the above, some Jews neither accept nor practice much of the above in their personal identities as Jews but still remain Jews.

Definitions: The Jews as a Minority Group

In this study, the Jews are considered to be not just an ethnic group but an ethnic minority group. As with the term "ethnic group," there is some disagreement and imprecision in the definitions scholars have given to the term "minority." It is also important to distinguish between different categories of minority groups. The Jews, for instance, represent a different category of minority in American society, than Blacks, Hispanics, or Native Americans.

Newman (1973) lists three criteria for a group to be considered a minority: first, it must vary from the social norms of society; second, it must be subordinate in power; and third, it must always number less than half of the population. Schermerhorn (1970), in labeling a minority group as one that is subordinate in both size and power, excludes Newman's first criterion. Ogbu (1978) has presented a useful typology for identifying the minority group that emphasizes and clarifies the element of power rather than size. He suggests that there are three types of minorities including (1) autonomous minorities, which are not totally subordinate and tend to be numerically smaller, (2) caste minorities, which are clearly subordinate to the dominant group, and (3) immigrant minorities, which fall somewhere between the first two groups and operate outside established definitions of social relations.

Working with these three definitions, the Jews are most accurately defined and understood as an autonomous ethnic minority group. The culture of the Jewish people is not dominant in American society, to some extent the norms of the Jews vary from the norms of American society, the Jews are numerically smaller than the majority, but, in many ways, notably socio-economically, they are not subordinate.

Intergroup Contact: Americanization

The Jewish people face the problem of maintaining and transmitting their cultural authenticity—perhaps even their very survival as an ethnic group—while living in a society whose dominant culture is different. Each minority group's response to intergroup relations is unique and is influenced and often determined by the majority group's changing attitudes and actions based on the interplay of a complex set of variables relating to intergroup contact. Three responses to ethnic minority-majority contact that are particularly relevant to the Jewish experience in America include Americanization, the melting pot, and cultural pluralism.

Americanization, or Anglo-conformity as some refer to it (Krug 1976), represents the desire to force all ethnic minority groups to conform to what is known as Anglo-Saxon culture. This is one of the approaches that Jews have feared threatens their survival. Although Anglo-conformity has not been able to succeed entirely, it has at times in American history been a concept with great popular support. Even in this century, Woodrow Wilson, while still President, said, "America does not consist of groups... A man who thinks of himself as belonging to a particular national group in America has not yet become an American." (Gordon 1964:101).

Newman (1973) places Anglo-conformity under the broad category of assimilation, in which a minority assumes the culture and other characteristics of the dominant group. Milton Gordon's (1964) well-known theory of assimilation suggests that there are several stages of assimilation that can occur, including cultural, structural, marital, identificational, attitude perceptional, behavioral receptional, and civic assimilation.

Gordon argues that once structural assimilation occurs, all other stages of assimilation follow. He states that the failure of Anglo-conformity to be more successful in America has been the result of the failure of structural assimilation to occur. Likewise, Gordon's analysis of the Jewish experience in America is that despite their having been culturally assimilated to a substantial degree, their strong independent structural network has accounted for their survival as an ethnic group. While Gordon's analysis is useful in setting out different categories of assimilation, he does not make allowances for a reversal of the assimilation process or for a group's possible return to cultural authenticity once the assimilation process has begun. (Newman 1973).

Intergroup Contact: The Melting Pot

The melting pot theory, calling for the fusion of cultures (Krug 1976) has two components, the permissive melting pot and the exclusivist melting pot (Castaneda 1974). The ideal of the permissive melting pot is the equal integration and melting of all ethnic groups in America in order to create a single but superior "American" group. In fact, many American Jews have welcomed this approach to intergroup relations as a way of achieving full acceptance and integration in American society. However, most Jewish leaders have viewed the permissive melting pot as a threat to the uniqueness of the Jewish character and tradition.

Other melting pot theorists have envisioned (some have feared) an exclusivist melting pot that would intentionally serve the very purposes of Anglo-conformity. Will Herberg (1955) wrote of his concern for this second type of melting pot, saying, "Our cultural assimilation has taken place not in a 'melting pot' but rather in a "transmuting pot' in which all ingredients have been transformed and assimilated to an idealized 'Anglo-Saxon model.'"

This exclusivist melting pot, much like Anglo-conformity, is precisely what those Jews concerned with Jewish disappearance through assimilation have feared.

Intergroup Contact: Cultural Pluralism

Cultural pluralism is the only model of ethnic minority-majority relations that is generally assumed to have the potential to allow for the full realization of ethnic group aspirations. As an ideal, it is a practice that acknowledges the differences among ethnic groups and at the same time affords equal status to them. Ethnic minority groups have often found that the theory of cultural pluralism has best suited ethnic minority interests. This study, however, raises questions as to whether there are limits to cultural pluralism that may prevent the full realization of ethnic group aspirations, at least in terms of ethnic authenticity and substance.

The condition of cultural pluralism desired by many ethnic groups was expressed by Berkson (1920:53) in the context of the Jewish people, as the "desire of the Jews to maintain their identity and to live the life of Jews in the midst of the social conditions of a divergent environment." Kallen believed that this response to majority-minority ethnic relations, what he called "Unity in Diversity" was in close accordance with the Declaration of Independence, represented the democratic ideals of the nation, and was best suited not just for the minority ethnic groups, but for the nation as a whole (Kallen 1956, 1924).

There are several closely linked interpretations of the meaning of cultural pluralism. Castaneda (1974) differentiates between two types in this category, mandatory and optional pluralism. He describes mandatory pluralism as a federation of independent national cultures within one State. More important to this study is optional pluralism, which differs, he says, in that it allows the individual the right to choose to assimilate while the individual's group maintains structural and cultural identity. Banks (1977) arrives at a term, pluralist-assimilationist, to describe his ideal type. His pluralism model allows for equal majority and minority rights, the realization of bicultural integrity and an interest in biculturalism on the part of both minority and majority peoples. Newman (1973) writes that the two major types of cultural pluralism that have occurred in U.S. history are most easily conceptualized in the terms, segregated pluralism and, more important to this study, integrated pluralism. By these terms he means societies in which groups either inhabit their own particular geographical area or intermix, respectively.

The Jews described in this study range in practice and attitude from an optional-integrated pluralism model to an integrated pluralist-assimilationist mode. They intermix geographically, desire equal majority and minority rights, and expect the group to maintain structural and cultural identity. While few Jews make a conscious decision to move toward assimilation (certainly not toward disappearance), what is problematic for the group is that their full integration into the majority society coincides with a loss of Jewish authenticity and substance. Banks' ideal, that allows for the realization of bicultural integrity is, unfortunately, not realized in this study of the Jews. It may be, that while cultural pluralism remains the best model of intergroup relations for ethnic minorities, the integrated model, whether optional or pluralist-assimilationist, has its limits beyond which its ideals cannot be achieved.

The Jewish School and Cultural Pluralism

Cultural Transmission and Schooling

The Jewish school is viewed in this study as a major focal point for initiating and responding to ethnic minority-majority contact and as an agency of substantial power for cultural transmission.

Spindler (1974) describes cultural transmission as the process by which "young humans come to want to act as they must act if the cultural system is to be maintained." Aberle (1961) adds that cultural transmission is those patterns of action which inculcate in individuals, the skills, motives, attitudes, and knowledge which are necessary for them to perform in present or future roles.

Proponents of both Anglo-conformity and cultural pluralism have tried to use the school to fit their own aims. Although unsuccessful in achieving complete assimilation, some people recognize the public school as being the major instrument of cultural assimilation in American society (Kopan 1974). Parsons (1959) writes that schooling in America is the focal socializing agency for those entering into first grade until their entry into the labor force. Carnoy (1974:330) states that "schools transfer culture and values and they channel children into its various roles." Dreeben (1968), in concurrence with the others, describes his theory of just how schools socialize normative behavior:

> In school, pupils participate in activities where they are expected to act as if they actually were conforming to these norms whether they actually accept them at a particular time or not. Through such participation, it is my belief, pupils will in time know their content, accept them as binding upon themselves, and act in accordance with them in appropriate situations.

During the waves of immigration into the U.S. at the turn of the twentieth century sentiment for Anglo-conformity was intense. One educator expressed that mood (Cubberly 1909:15) telling how the schools could work towards that end:

> Everywhere these people tend to settle in groups or settlements, and to set up here their national manners, customs, and observances. Our task is to break up these groups or settlements, to assimilate and amalgamate these people as part of our American race, and to implant in their children, so far as can be done, the Anglo-Saxon conception of righteousness, law and order, and popular government...

Cultural Pluralism and Schools

Advocates of cultural pluralism believe that the educational goal of public school children in America should be that of learning to function and to contribute to more than one cultural world (Castaneda 1974B). Some of these advocates, however, have been critical of some of the programs that have emerged in the public schools in the name of cultural pluralism (Macias 1975). While some continue to support the idea of working through the public schools, others argue that the goals of cultural pluralism simply cannot be achieved through the public schools alone.

The alternative that these critics arrived at was the creation of the "ethnic schools." These were to be schools that had as their function the "organization and orientation of the ethnic filial generations to the linguistic, historical, and religious aspects of the ancestral society' (Warner and Srole 1945). It was also hoped that such schools would instill in youth a positive self-concept and would make school children feel proud of their ethnicity (Lewin 1970). On the goal of the Jewish school, Dushkin (1966) wrote to the point, saying, "The primary purpose of Jewish education in the diaspora is to teach life to Jewish children in accordance with the Jewish way of living...'

The two main varieties of ethnic schools that emerged were the day school and the supplementary school. The day school, which has at times met with resistance from local and state governments under the guise of "improper standards" (Hostetler and Huntington 1971) is, according to some of its proponents, the only way to insure proper ethnic training. Others, such as the proponents of the supplementary school, disagree that the day school is the best or "only" method, arguing that the day school does not provide for sufficient multi-ethnic contact.

Stating that the supplementary school is able to provide the best of both worlds, Berkson (1920:170) writes, "Each system of schools would insure the integrity of the community which supports it; the public schools would further the society of the state; the religious and ethnic schools, the society of minority communities." However, critics argue that the hoped for harmonious balance of cultural identification through the existence of the supplementary schools has not occurred. Instead, they state that what has happened for the advocates of these schools is a major clash over their desire for full integration into American society and their desire for continued ethnic survival, and an uncomfortable ambivalence as to how to confront the problem (Elazar 1973).

Background of the Jewish School

The Jewish afternoon school is an example of the supplementary ethnic school. Although the history of this type of school dates back only to the first decades of the twentieth century, most Jews point to the command of the Bible, "And you shall teach it to your children" as the origin of their interest in education. Certainly, the Jewish people are proud to be known as the "People of the Book."

The first recorded history of Jewish education in the U.S. dates back to 1731 in New York. For the next century, the Spanish and Portugese Jewish immigrants continued to establish day schools and, later, supplementary schools as well (Winter 1966). In the mid-nineteenth century many of the German-Jewish immigrants experimented with Sunday schools that met only one morning a week. However, some among this group of settlers were appalled at the decline in religious observance in America and organized their own day schools as well. The east European immigration, occurring at the end of the eighteen-hundreds, brought to the twentieth century a variety of types of Jewish instruction. Among others, there existed instruction by private tutors, one hour per week Sunday schools, Talmud Torah schools serving poorer children, and the rigid and more intensive school known as the Cheder, which in the U.S. never achieved the prominence it had enjoyed in Europe. Despite the variety of channels for Jewish education, Winter (1966) reports that "Jewish education, at the turn of the twentieth century, was in a deplorable condition. Religious instruction was inadequate, inefficient, or non-existent... The majority of Jewish children received no religious instruction at all."

One important factor in the difficulty Jews had in sustaining Jewish education in the U.S. emerged in the form of free public education. Ackerman (1977) recounts that the "overwhelming majority of Jews in mid-nineteenth century America welcomed the opportunity provided by the public school and were among its most ardent supporters. Even statements such as that of Horace Mann—'Our system earnestly inculcates all the Christian morals; it founds its morals on the basis of religion'—which reflected the influence and power of the Protestant establishment in the conduct of the local school systems, did not stem the stream of Jewish children entering the public school." The East European immigrants arriving at the close of the nineteenth century, "had come from countries where Jewish learning, while not compulsory, was universal. In the United States, however, as a symbol of their freedom, they immediately enrolled their children in the public schools, and under the stress of economic and social conditions, they were often forced to neglect the Jewish education of their children" (Winter 1966). Gartner (1969) adds that Jews' enthusiasm for public education at the expense of Jewish education was in line with their concurrence with the goal of "Americanization." Gartner writes:

> As they soon came to believe, Jewish children could best become loyal and fully accepted Americans by mingling freely in public school with children of all religions and social classes. Sectarian Jewish education suggested undesirable, even dangerous separatism.

By the end of the first quarter of the twentieth century, however, Jewish sentiment changed and an increasing number of Jews became advocates of the ideals of cultural pluralism. Fed by the essays of Kallen in 1915 (see Kallen 1924) and the writings of Berkson in 1920, men like Samson Benderly created a system of complementary afternoon schools whose basic structure continues today (Winter 1966).

Research and Analysis of Jewish Schools

Recent studies on Jewish afternoon schools have looked for the long-term effect that Jewish schooling had on its students. Their results have not been particularly encouraging. Dashefsky and Shapiro (1974) found that through the social and substantive interaction that occurs in the afternoon school, Jewish children were being taught how to be Jewish both behaviorally and cognitively. The effect of such teaching was described as a stable factor but not a major independent factor in Jewish identification or, in the authors' words, "mild, but lasting." Himmelfarb's research (1975) found that while attendance at Jewish afternoon school did increase one's adult religious involvement beyond the level obtained by those with no Jewish schooling, such an increase could be demonstrated only among those who attended afternoon school for at least twelve years. Finally, Bock's study

(1977) concurred that "hours of instruction" was the best predictive measure for most conceptions of Jewish identification, adding that a minimum of roughly 1,000 hours of instruction was necessary before schooling could begin to substantially affect Jewish identification.

Many of the recent analyses and reflections on Jewish schooling are harsh in their criticism, discussing a wide range of problems. Some of the problems commonly mentioned are a shortage of qualified personnel due to low pay and only part-time work, insufficient community financing, poor instructional methods and materials, poor choice of meeting time, and unrealistic expectations for such short instructional time periods (Ackerman 1969). In a summary report on Jewish education and Jewish identity (Sidorsky 1977), a task force of the American Jewish Committee reported that "there is a widespread sentiment that much of Jewish education in the United States has been a failure...(charges) included the assertion that 'graduates of most Jewish schools are functionally illiterate in Judaism and not clearly positive in attitudinal identification.'" Himmelfarb (1975) adds to this list other problems, such as a lack of parental interest, a lack of neighborhood reinforcement for Jewish schooling, and a lack of seriousness about the school. Silberman (1976) even suggests that Jewish education today may very well be undermining or at least weakening commitment to Jewish life because of students' negative experiences in Jewish schools. His analysis of the current problem of Jewish schooling, similar to Kallen's analysis in 1939 (Kallen 1954), is that Jewish educators have failed to take into account the changing environment in which Jewish life is being lived.

Despite these criticisms of the school, the concern for its continued existence and the widespread belief that Jewish schooling still is or can be a factor closely tied to Jewish survival and Jewish authenticity do not appear to have diminished. Many in the "survival" category still agree with Wirth's statement (1943) that "education has been one of the prime forces making for the survival for the Jews." There is a persistent feeling that through Jewish schooling it is possible at the very least to "innoculate the next generation with that minimum of religious practice and belief considered necessary to keep alive a level of Jewish self-consciousness that will hold the line against assimilation." (Rosenthal 1970:150). At the other end, there is the hope among those searching for substance (Dushkin and Engelman 1959) that Jewish education can enable American Jews to reach all four levels of living and being as described in Hassidic literature: identification, fellowship and participation, culture and knowledge, and finally, ethical living.

Chapter Two

METHODOLOGY

Ethnographic Research

This study is an attempt to present an ethnography of one Jewish afternoon school (Schoem 1983a). Spindler (1970) writes that "An ethnography is a report and interpretation of events that never again will be repeated, that occurred in a time forever gone. But the class of events, the categories of behavior, are repeated endlessly." Ethnographic research is not typical of most educational research although it has a long and respected tradition in the field of anthropology. However, as scholars from the fields of anthropology and education have come closer together (La Belle 1972), the use of ethnography in educational research has increased (see Wolcott 1973; King 1967). Ethnographic research differs from traditional research in that the research problem under study is usually not definitively formulated at the outset but rather develops throughout the course of the study (Everhart 1976). Cassell (1978) writes that "Rather than seeking to 'measure and predict,' its primary aim is to 'understand' the phenomena of the social world. It is open-ended." Other social scientists add that ethnographic research is best used for discovering the unexpected and for generating hypotheses (Byrne 1974; Lutz and Ramsey 1974; Overholt & Stallings, 1976).

According to John Goodlad (1977), such an approach to educational research is needed because research regarding educational outcomes has been so pervasive that information regarding what goes on in schools is extremely scarce. Goodlad (1977:3) writes:

> To carry on a serious dialogue about, let alone to seek to change, American schooling or simply the local elementary school without a rather substantial body of the information implied seems somewhat bizarre. And yet, to do so is virtually a national pastime. In our pseudo-wisdom, we know what schools need without knowing what they already have, and we know what to put into them without knowing what needs to be replaced.

The Need for Ethnographic Research in Studies of the Jewish Community

Research on Jewish education and Jewish identity has been far more limited that studies of public education, yet the research that has taken place has generally followed the pattern that Goodlad criticizes. As already noted, there have been studies in Jewish education of enrollment trends (Lang 1968) and of educational effect (Dashefsky and Shapiro 1974; Himmelfarb 1974; Bock 1976); there have been discussions about theories of Jewish education (Fox 1973); but there have not been studies looking at what goes on in Jewish schools (see Ackerman 1978; for exceptions, see Lipnick 1976; Wolfson 1974). Similarly there have been recent studies of the Jewish community looking at identity, change, assimilation, and renewal (Cohen 1988, 1983; Goldscheider 1986; Goldscheider & Zuckerman 1984; Silberman 1985; Waxman 1983) but there have not been qualitative studies looking inside the quantitative measurements to fully understand what the data means to the members of the Jewish community who provided it. Taking note of this problem, the colloquium on Jewish Education and Jewish Identity commented (Sidorksy 1977) that "on any examination of the goals of an educational institution, there is an important distinction between the formulated, explicit set of aims and the actual, tacit goals which only a kind of "anthropology of the classroom can uncover."

An Holistic View of the Jewish School and the Community

A second characteristic of ethnography is that it attempts to go beyond the more formalistic treatment of a social phenomenon or setting to present a more holistic view (Spindler 1971; Everhart, 1976). This study proposed to investigate the entire community of the Jewish afternoon school, operationally defined to include students, parents, staff (including teachers, principal, and rabbi), school board, and a mix of other interested parties. In addition to gathering and analyzing data on the behavior and activities of the school community, it looked into the attitudes, expectations, and assessments of these groups regarding the Jewish school, an area in which there exists almost no information (Fox 1973; for exceptions, see Dushkin and Engelman 1959; Stone and Newman 1975). It studied the relationship of the school to the lives of the community members of the school as that relationship was perceived by the community. In addition, it examined that relationship in the context of schooling's social functions and, also, in the context of school community members' Jewish identity in a non-Jewish America.

Furthermore, the study proposed to consider the school from what might be described as a modified structural functional viewpoint. The study accepted the premise that some degree of human action occurs through the process of symbolic interaction (Blumer 1969). This is the process in which individuals become involved in interactions, interpret meanings and actions, adjust their "cognitive maps" (Gearing 1975) as a result of their interpretations, and then act on the basis of such newly formed "cognitive maps." However, the study also accepted the position that the process of symbolic interaction takes place within a framework and under the constraints of social roles and social structures.

A final characteristic of ethnography is that its perspective of the problem is commonly expansive and complex and that the written account is subsequently in-depth and rich in descriptive detail. As a result of the use of these approaches to the study, it was expected that a holistic picture of the afternoon school would emerge.

Qualitative Methodology

Qualitative methods are generally credited with providing the desired in-depth perspective (Everhart 1976; Lofland 1971; Vidich and Shapiro 1955). As this study employed qualitative methods, including participant observation, in-depth interviewing, and a review of curricular materials and documents, it was anticipated that an in-depth understanding of the Jewish afternoon school would be achieved.

Qualitative research is said to be a humanistic methodology because it provides a reasonable substitute for "face-to-face" knowing by getting close to the data and by being factual, descriptive, and quotive in an attempt to represent people on their own terms (Lofland 1971). Qualitative research is highly regarded (Dean et al. 1969) for its non-standardization and adaptive techniques that allow for flexibility in purpose, methods, and analysis. In a study that desires an in-depth perspective such flexibility is a necessity. Zelditch (1962) writes that qualitative methods are the best methods for gathering data on incidents and histories, and on norms and statuses, all of which were crucial to this ethnographic report. He suggests the use of participant observation for the former, and informant interviewing for the latter. In this study both methods were used.

Entree

Entree is an important aspect of the research because of the importance of securing one's choice of research site and because of the initial impressions that are made. In this study, preparations were made several months in advance to study an elementary afternoon school attached to a conservative synagogue in a suburban area. This type of school was desired because, as noted earlier, it is statistically typical of a large percentage of Jewish schools in America (Lang 1968). As was the case with this school, the largest percentage of students attending Jewish schools nationally (44.4%) were enrolled in 2-5 day a week supplementary schools (Rockowitz and Lang 1976). Also, the largest number of Jewish schools appeared to fall within the range of 100-299 students, as did this school. (Data comes from preliminary statistical sample used in update of Rockowitz and Lang 1976). Finally, the greatest number of conservative congregations who had such schools had a membership size of 100-249 families such as was the case in this study (Friedman 1979). The researcher met at length with the principal of the chosen suburban school, explaining his personal background, his goals for the research, the methods of research to be used, and his expectations of school personnel with regard to the research. The researcher was then given permission to study the school with the enthusiastic support of the principal and rabbi. In return for this permission, the researcher agreed to provide the school with the results of the study when they became available. It should be noted, too, that within the text of this study all personal names referred to are pseudonyms.

Role Clarification

In such a personalized type of research, mutually satisfactory impressions as well as subsequent relationships are critical for establishing and maintaining cooperation and support for the research. During the early stages of research it is also important for the researcher to clarify his/her role to the subjects of the research in a manner that will facilitate complete and accurate data collection. In this ethnography, it was important for the researcher to be identified as an independent researcher and personality and not to be over-identified with any of the school groups. This facet of the research was important in order to insure that all the subjects would feel free to speak openly and behave as usual. It was also important for the researcher to stress the significance of the study for the participants so that they would be desirous of speaking openly to the researcher.

At every opportunity the researcher introduced himself to individuals or groups of the school community, explaining his presence and the purpose of his research. Despite this, there was some limited role confusion early in the study. Some students showed concern that the researcher was a teacher and some teachers looked to the researcher as an evaluator. However, the researcher took note of this confusion and acted to correct it. He did not give teachers critical feedback on their teaching methods that they frequently but anxiously requested, he refused to act as a substitute teacher even in emergency situations and he would not react in a disciplinary fashion to what was considered unacceptable student behavior (the researcher was tested by students on this issue).

Participant Observation

The researcher used the role model of participant-as-observer (Gold 1958) in this study. In this model there is no role-pretense as in the model of complete participant, for the participant-as-observer is known to the participants as the researcher. This role affords the researcher the opportunity to ask questions about people and events, to conduct interviews, to work with informants with a degree of openness, and to give full attention to observations. In observations of interaction in the classroom in this study, the researcher had to attempt to become such a natural part of of the setting that what behavior was observed was neither caused by nor particular to the researcher's presence. There were several independent and complimentary comments made to the researcher regarding his ability to blend into the background, remain neutral, and be unobtrusive. However, the researcher also noted during the year a high degree of introspection and critical analysis in the school community that may have been prompted by the researcher's presence.

The researcher had to be careful in judging the accuracy of informants' data and of becoming over-identified with the informants. The researcher also had to be concerned with the possibility that personal bias would influence his observations and analysis. In addition, there was also a concern that the researcher's familiarity with Jewish schooling might prejudice his thoughts. As a result, the researcher took care not to take sides on public issues, sometimes risking the anger of one informant or another for not showing more support. He also hoped that the constant process of collection and analysis of data and the constant comparison of reported behavior would give him the opportunity to check for accuracy, to restructure questions, to redirect limiting perceptions and to reduce the influence of bias to a minimum (Becker and Geer 1957).

Data Collection and Analysis

The specific method of data collection for this study included observations, review of documents, and interviews. Notebook and pen always in hand, the researcher observed the students of one Jewish afternoon school, grades four through seven, for a period of ten months, extending from September to June. This group was chosen over younger students because of their better developed verbal abilities and greater awareness of the world about them. High school aged students were not chosen because most students in Jewish afternoon schools discontinue their studies at age thirteen. Observations for one week or less were also made of students in the younger grades of this school as well as of students in the high school program. The principal of the school was closely observed or "shadowed" (see Wolcott 1973) for at least two sessions. The researcher also observed regular school board meetings, relevant synagogue board meetings, staff meetings, and staff and parent meetings. He attended school and synagogue activities, participated in carpools, and was present at innumerable informal events such as office talk, pre-class teacher conversations, student recess activities, post-meeting politics, dinner talk, etc. Finally, for the purpose of comparison, observations for one week or less were made at two reform and one orthodox afternoon school, as well as at two non-Jewish ethnic afternoon school programs.

The researcher also examined and analyzed curricular materials, memos, signs, posters, letters, budget reports, and other school documents that were made available to him. It was expected that this activity would provide additional information on a variety of topics.

Finally, the researcher conducted in-depth interviews with members of the school community (see Table 1 below for breakdown). Theoretical sampling was used to determine who would be interviewed, employing the techniques of quota sampling, snowball sampling, and deviant sampling. The researcher employed various interview techniques including four styles of questions that Strauss (1969) has suggested: 1) devil's advocate, 2) hypothetical, 3) posing the ideal, 4) testing propositions. Informal interviewing was constantly used by the researcher as an integral part of participant observation.

Table 1
Numerical Breakdown of Formal Interviews
Total Interviewed/Total Number

Students	Male	Female	Total	%Total
4th Grade	8/9	5/9	13/18	72
5th Grade	5/15	3/8	8/23	35
6th Grade	4/16	1/4	5/20	25
7th Grade	6/12	6/10	12/22	55
Total Numbers	23/52	15/31	38/83	45.8
Total %	60.5%/62.7%	39.5%/37.3%	100%/100%	

Total Interviewed/Total Number

			%Total
Staff	16	21	76.2
Parents of Students grades 4-7	20	70	28.6
School Board	6	12 (Approx.)	50
Others	6		

Totals -	Students -	38
	School Adults -	36
	Others -	6
		80

Note: Student interviews ranged from ten to forty-five minutes, increasing markedly in the seventh grade and with particular individuals. Adult interviews ranged from forty-five minutes to two hours. Some fourth grade students were interviewed in pairs. The number given for parents interviewed was determined by counting "one" for each different family, regardless of the number of parents in the family or at the interview.

In qualitative research, the processes of collection and analysis of data are concurrent. The data gathered in this study from the variety of methods already discussed here were constantly being reviewed and integrated. For instance, as Goodlad (1977) suggests, study of the curriculum can be looked at as ideal (on paper), perceived (teacher and parents), operational (as observed), and experienced (students). In the process of the data being reviewed, integrated, and analyzed, the researcher attempted to develop meaningful analyses and hypotheses about the information and its relation to the total picture of the school. This constant analysis, coupled with the flexibility inherent in the methodology, allowed the researcher to become increasingly directed in his observations and interviews as the research progressed.

Special Notes on the Research Study

The Use of Children in Research

Throughout the course of the study, the researcher was frequently admonished by adults of the community, i.e. parents, staff, school board, etc., not to pay heed to comments their children might make. Many suggested that the students' complaints and stories about the afternoon school were just "kids' talk." One parent related that "everyday he [her son] comes up with "I"m not going next year!" However she felt that there was peer pressure that forced him to say he didn't like it, and she, in fact, believed that he did like school. Parents never suggested to the researcher that their own opinions might be swayed by various influences. More to the point, another parent stated, "I don't usually listen to kids because they see things from a different point of view." While the researcher agreed that the students often had a different point of view, or at least a kind of logic that differed from their parents, he chose not to disregard their comments but rather record and consider their perspective with as much diligence as was done for adults. It is interesting to note that in the study the children's description of classroom behavior and interaction proved on many occasions to be more in line with the researcher's observations than the descriptions provided by other adults. Furthermore, the adults would often make policy decisions based on incomplete impressions of classroom life, all the while refuting out of hand their best witnesses.

Researching One's Own Group

Being a Jew and an educator, it was necessary for the researcher to be aware of some special circumstances in his relationship to members of the community of the Jewish afternoon school. As a Jew, the researcher was taken to be an "insider" and it was assumed that he would exhibit normative Jewish behavior, however undefined. Any deviant behavior could not be explained away by the naivete of an "outside researcher." In addition, the researcher had to be very alert to the subtleties of issues not related to education or identity yet highly sensitive and hotly debated within the Jewish community. It was important that the researcher participate in these discussions, but that he always be careful not to offend possible informants.

As an educator known to the principal and some teachers as one who had experience teaching, developing curriculum, and consulting, a different problem arose. Members of the educational staff frequently approached the researcher for suggestions, criticisms, and other evaluative advice. However, the researcher was sensitive to the anxiety with which this evaluation was sought, and could forsee the negative consequences that might result (Khlief 1974), should he succumb to their requests. As a result, the researcher's strategy was not to give any advice or evaluative information, but rather to offer only non-substantive feedback and support. Despite the burden of these added precautions, the researcher was aware that the fact of his being Jewish and having had extensive educational experience was a crucial element in gaining such enthusiastic acceptance to conduct the study at this school.

The Difficulty of Maintaining a Distanced Involvement

Miller (1952) has presented a theoretical paper on the dangers of over-rapport in field research, and Beals (1970) and Boissevain (1970) have discussed how over-involvement affected their own field studies. Yet, despite the obvious problems inherent in over-involvement, the researcher found that it was not an easy matter to maintain a kind of "distanced involvement." In conflicts between teacher and parent, student and teacher, or principal and school board, the researcher was frequently asked his opinion, but as a policy he begged to refrain from entering the fracas. At hours-long meetings of the congregation board, the researcher sat silently taking notes of discussions which sometimes included personal insults and emotional tirades. Similarly, the researcher patiently observed hours of what were sometimes very boring classes with only indirect witicisms as comments to the teachers. The researcher found it unnatural, not at all easy, but finally, very very wise to do as he did. Some community members even mentioned to the researcher that they had rarely seen such controlled behavior as he had demonstrated.

Community Interest in the Research and Researcher

Although it is not infrequent that a community welcomes a researcher into its midst, the enthusiasm shown toward this researcher and the interest shown his research were beyond any of the researcher's expectations. The initial enthusiastic permission granted by the principal and later graciously extended by the rabbi was just the beginning. Throughout the year students would rush up to the researcher asking, "When are you going to visit our class?" and "Will you interview me? Please?" Teachers, either in carpools or over dinner, would constantly ask the researcher to confirm or disconfirm their own theories about Jewish education. Many parents seemed genuinely grateful to be interviewed and to have an opportunity to contribute data to the research. Many were concerned with how their school "measured up" to others. One parent quietly whispered to the researcher as he was leaving her home after an interview, "Actually, I couldn't wait for you to come to our house so I could hear what my husband had to say. _____ (a friend's name) told me that she and her husband had learned so many things about one another after your interview and they spent the whole night talking about them after you left."

Of course, such a degree of interest can result in what McCall (1969) has described as "reactive observation." The researcher noted what he felt was an undue amount of introspection and analysis with which the researcher was concerned. Whether this actually resulted in much or any change at the school is hard to judge. However, it seems that the problem of limiting this type of reactive behavior while maintaining interest and enthusiasm among the research population is an issue that will require further consideration in future research.

PART II
IDENTITY AND COMMUNITY

Chapter Three

THE ANTI-ANTI-SEMITES AND THE NON-NON-JEWS

Questions of identity and identification are concerns of many in this complex, modern world. Yet the ethnic minority in a pluralistic society bears the burden of an additional and important concern in this domain. It must reckon with the difficult question of ethnic identity and ethnic identification as well. So it is not surprising that in the case of the Jew, questions of Jewish identity and Jewish identification have been increasingly problematic and are of growing concern.

The terms "identity" and "identification" have often been used interchangeably, albeit with some ambiguity. Indeed there are some similarities in meaning and there do exist linkages between the two terms. According to Dashefsky (1972:240), "identity is the sector of the personal system that maintains personal continuity through the coherent organization of information about the individual." He notes the linkage between identity and identification by viewing identification as a process upon which identity can be elaborated as well as a product with which one may identify oneself. The important difference in identity and identification, as implied in Dashefsky's definition, is that while identity refers to something within an individual, identification assumes the presence of an outside source in addition to the individual, i.e. one has one's own identity, but one identifies with some other person, group, etc. The importance of this distinction becomes apparent as one begins to examine the Jewish identity and Jewish identification of the people at Shalom School. Whereas these people proudly identified with the Jewish group, they, at the same time, exhibited ambivalence, confusion, conflict, and an emptiness in their Jewish identity.

Jewish Identification

Stone (1962) suggests that there are two processes of identification, those being "identification of" and "identification with." The people of Shalom School identified with the Jewish group in both respects as they 1) recognized the Jewish group as a socially defined category of people and they 2) linked themselves with this group. Lindesmith and Strauss (1968) have suggested that this linkage can be either symbolic and/or organizational. For the parents of students in the school, the linkage included both aspects. They thought of themselves as being part of the Jewish group (symbolic), and they had formally joined the Jewish synagogue (organizational). The children attending the school shared the symbolic linkage but were in most cases not given a choice in their organizational association with the school. While all of the teachers were also symbolically linked with the Jewish group, their organizational associations were varied, and a few teachers resisted that association entirely outside of their tie with the Jewish school.

Recognition and Pride for the Jewish Group

In recognizing the Jewish group as a category of people, there were several key elements that were used recurringly to define them. The people of Shalom School spoke of the Jewish group as one with a grand, albeit persecuted history. They added that it had developed through history a rich religious and cultural tradition that included numerous holidays, that it had a concern for Israel, and a deep and constant concern for threats to its survival. Their image of the Jewish group included a wide spectrum of Jewish peoples with their accompanying differences in thoughts, values, and practices.

Kelman (1977) has illustrated that the recognition of a group's identity does not imply uniformity of acceptance, involvement, or commitment to that group by individuals who identify with the group. Kelman writes that individual adoption of elements of a group's identity may come in the form of compliance, identification, or internalization. Kelman favors internalization, which he describes as the acceptance of group identity based on a consideration of it in terms of the individual's own values. However, the people of Shalom School appeared to adopt the group's identity more in terms of identification and compliance, and particularly in terms of compliance. Kelman describes identification as a high affective, though inflexible and unreflective, involvement in a group's identity based on either pride or guilt. "Compliance," writes Kelman (1977:20), "may lead to ritualistic practice, lacking in personal involvement and conviction; or to a nominal acceptance of group identity, devoid of substantive content, and subject to mobilization only in response to threats of group survival."

Indeed, considerable variation existed among the people of Shalom School in the degree of acceptance, involvement, and commitment with which people identified with the Jewish group. Yet there was no one who did not identify with the group. Furthermore, there was a widespread feeling of pride that accompanied this identification. It was only a rare student who told the researcher that "being Jewish doesn't matter to me" or "I wouldn't care whether I was Jewish or not."

The Anti-Anti-Semites and Survival

Clearly, however, the strongest factors in maintaining Jewish identification at Shalom School seemed to come from a fear and hatred for anti-semites and a deep and penetrating concern for Jewish survival. These intertwined factors, far beyond anything else, were offered as the reasons for people's strong identification with the Jewish group. For some, their concern for anti-semitism and survival came as a result of historical knowing but not as a reaction to particular incidents one experienced in this community. One parent commented:

We know we're Jewish. We know a lot about it. We accept it. We have the feeling that we belong—a sense of responsibility; a special little group that has to cling to each other otherwise you might not exist; feeling a part of the six million,[1] Israel. You know you are special because of persecution and it could happen to you.

That feeling of being special because of the group's record for survival was widespread. At times, people spoke in terms of survival for survival's sake. One student spoke of this feeling in terms akin to an endangered species. He said, "It's sort of an honor to be Jewish, because there aren't many Jews left." It was also the students who seemed to experience more frequently events considered anti-Semitic. A not very uncommon example was given by one student:

Other kids bug me because I'm Jewish. They say 'Where you going, Jew, to the Temple?' and things like that. And it bothers me.

Similarly, a mother related the following incident that involved her son.

A couple of weeks ago at recess a bunch of boys came up to Josh at recess and ganged up on him and started shouting 'Jew, kinky-haired Jew! And Josh came home and said, 'Gee, Mom, I'm really glad to be Jewish but it's hard sometimes.'

In the classroom, teachers frequently related stories or showed examples of anti-semitism in the community. Teachers would bring to class, for instance, pictures or headlines from local city newspapers and explain the anti-semitism implicit in them. One teacher came to class one day telling how that very day he had registered a perfect score on a food manager's test except for three questions on pork (a forbidden food in Jewish dietary laws). He concluded his story in class by emphasizing that one needs to be careful of anti-semites and anti-semitism in all places and in all types of activities, implying that the test had been written by anti-semites.

Indeed, Jewish identification in the minds of the people of Shalom School appeared foremost as an issue of group survival. There were other reasons for identification as well, such as a pride in the group's history, and a good feeling about undefined Jewish values, the Jewish religion, and Israel, which for a minority of people seemed important, too. However, the issue of Jewish self-preservation clearly seemed to predominate (see Diagram A) as the following words of one parent indicate:

Though we may be scattered and not really practice or stand on the soap box and say, 'I am a Jew,' when it comes down to the crunch, where one has to declare themselves, the Jew will be there.

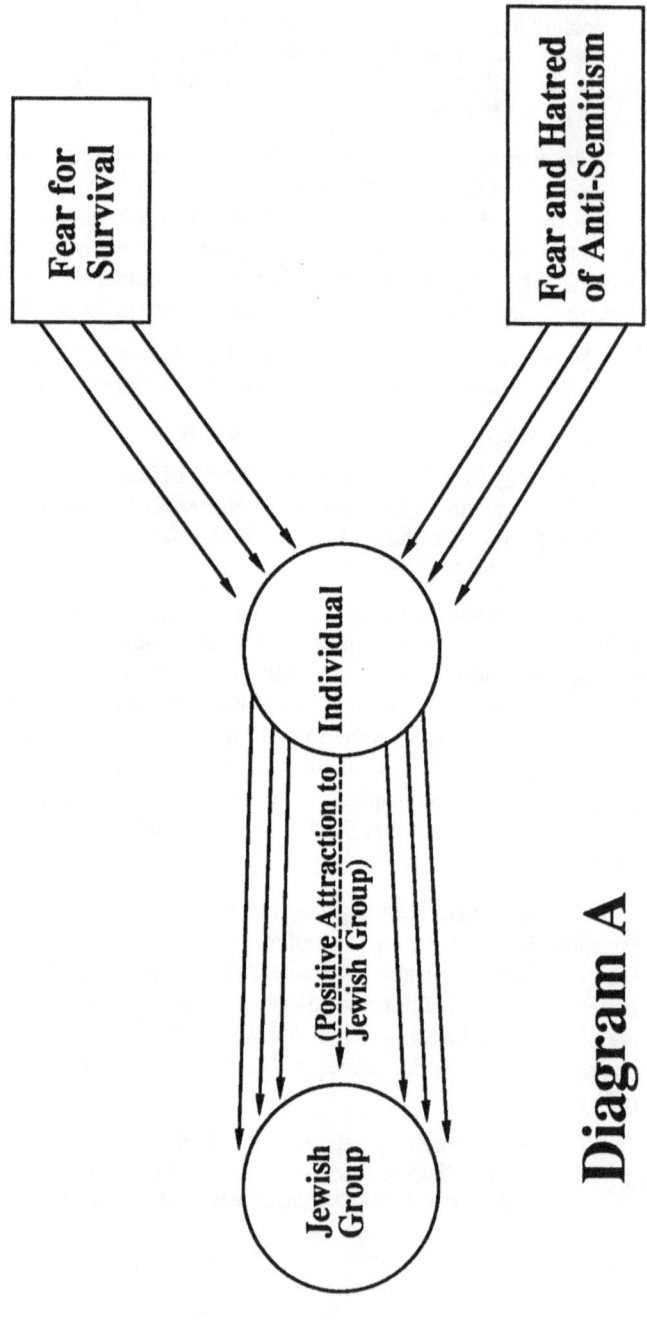

Jewish Identity—Behavioral

Many of the people of the Shalom School spoke of their Jewish identity in terms of their Jewish behaviors, observances, and practices. As will be seen in the case of their attitudinal identity, their behavior seemed strongly influenced by the secular environment in which they lived. While these people did do what could be described as Jewish behavior, overall it was much less than they imagined it to be and it was something that was rarely integrated into their daily routine.

Daily Routines

The parents of Shalom School lived in upper middle class suburban towns. None of the parents whom the researcher interviewed lived in apartments. Their homes were always fashionably decorated, frequently with large and elaborately furnished kitchens, dining rooms, and living rooms (these were the areas where the interview was usually held). Some of the homes had swimming pools, many had front and back yards, and almost all had garages, many for two cars.

The men in the community were almost exclusively white collar and professional workers. There were many doctors, lawyers, and business people. Many of the women in the community described themselves as housewives, but several also worked, although almost always in lower status positions than their spouses. Looking at sixteen couples who were interviewed, the occupational breakdown followed this pattern:

Men	Women
6 - Medical Professionals (4 physicians, 1 ophthalmologist,	9 - Housewives
	4 - Teachers
1 - Pharmacist	1 - Registered Nurse
6 - Business & industrial management	1 - Medical Technician
2 - Engineers	1 - Taxpayer Service Representative
1 - Private business owner	
1 - Lawyer	

The day-to-day routine of parents of Shalom School was dominated by work considerations but allowed for some family time and recreational activities such as television, movies, dinner out, athletics, etc. Some parents were involved in Jewish organizational activities usually but not exclusively associated with Shalom Synagogue. The women who were housewives took responsibility for shopping and other household responsibilities as well as for chauffeuring children to various school and after-school activities.

The teachers at Shalom School kept busy in a number of ways. Some of the female teachers were housewives. Other teachers, both male and female, held a variety of part-time jobs in addition to teaching at the Jewish school. Finally, there were a few teachers who were full-time university students and some of these teachers held additional part-time jobs as well.

Students at Shalom School spent most of their weekday time in secular school. However, many students were busy almost every day after school in organized activities such as sports, music, dance, and Jewish school. Many of the sixth and seventh grade students were becoming increasingly interested in social activities. Some of the students also belonged to Jewish activity groups which met approximately twice per month. The students were highly interested in a current wave of media spectaculars on outer-space and futuristic technology.

"Stepping Out to be Jewish"

At one extreme of the Shalom School community was a small minority who felt that their Jewishness permeated their every action and thought in life. This feeling was expressed as follows by one parent:

> My Judaism is a constant part of my life. I am very emotional about it. It affects me ethnically, morally, culturally - every aspect of my life. I can always count on it. If you strip away everything, I still have my Jewishness.

However, for the great majority of the Shalom School community, their Jewishness, particularly in terms of behavior, was a facet of life that was increasingly less time-consuming and kept distinctly separate from their normative routine. Some people bemoaned the fact that they were not as behaviorally Jewish as they would have liked. Yet even among this group the perceived pressures not to behave Jewishly were overwhelming. One such women lamented:

> The subtle pressures of Americana are too strong—but there are no laws to stop you—you can do whatever you want... Not doing these things means I'm giving up some of my Judaism. To me, Judaism is ritual, as well. It's everything combined, everything I've learned—because I used to feel very deeply that this was the right way and the only way. But now, every time I give in a little, everyone applauds me, 'Oh good! Now you're becoming Americanized!' But I don't know if that's good—I don't like it.

More typical of the majority was the lack of concern that they were doing less Jewish behaviors. One man who boasted of his priorities reflected the attitude of many others. He said:

> I guess if there weren't so many pressures and directions - what with work and bills and taxes and weeds—we might sit down with books and read about Judaism. But hell, we'd rather watch the Super Bowl.

The types of Jewish behavior or observance listed by the people of Shalom School were most often extracurricular to their normal routines. Yet even the listed behaviors were not adhered to on a consistent basis. For example, although many parents spoke of lighting candles on Sabbath evening, few said they did this regularly, and frequently comments by a spouse or a child suggested to the researcher that a false impression of regular observance was being given. Even fewer families had regular Sabbath dinners, often giving way to a night for social activities. The observance of Kashrut, the Jewish dietary rules, was ignored by most and followed by others in a very "watered down" fashion. One student who told the researcher that he "kept Kosher" explained his observance as "We eat bagels and cream cheese every Sunday morning." Parents who claimed to observe Jewish holidays, it was found upon further elaboration, often did not attend services, did not have special meals, did not light candles or do any action that could be described as "observing." Observed attendance at Friday night and Saturday morning services showed that gathering the required minimum of ten people was not to be taken for granted except for special events such as a Bar/Bat Mitzvah[2] or a school presentation. Hanukah, because of its competition with Christmas, with the observance of candle lighting and present giving, seemed to be the most widely celebrated holiday during the school year.

Perhaps the most frequent and consistent Jewish behavior for the children, staff, and mothers of Shalom was the school itself. The staff and children were, of course, the central characters at the school building and were present during school hours; the mothers organized their time so that they could transport their children to the school and back home. Except for a few isolated cases, there were no other Jewish activities, programs, causes, or observances that were adhered to in such a manner.

However, even in regularly attending Shalom School, this Jewish behavior represented a kind of "stepping out" of one's routine of life to provide some small link with one's heritage (see Diagram B). Each of the various Jewish behaviors that people identified to the researcher and claimed to do or not do, infrequently or on a regular basis, were not a part of their present flow of life but rather were a connection with the past or with something outside of their lives. For many of these people, their Jewishness was positive and important, but at the same time historical. There was a strong sense that while Judaism's strength was its history, that very history simply did not transfer meaningfully into the lives of Jews today. To at least one student, the feeling that Judaism was unable to penetrate the present style in suburban life in America was a strong indication that Judaism was becoming or had become outdated. A high school student at Shalom School stated her concern for this matter in the following way:

> I think Judaism is kind of dead... All of the stories were written in the past, all the prophets. It's just like a history book, but the history isn't continuing. No one is saying, y'know, they're not writing about the Inquisition or World War II. It's not part of the Bible so it's not a continuing history. So, in that respect, it died, and the only thing continuing now are the traditions and the rituals that we derived a long time ago from the Talmud; and that's why I think it's dying—it's just the traditions.

30   Ethnic Survival in America

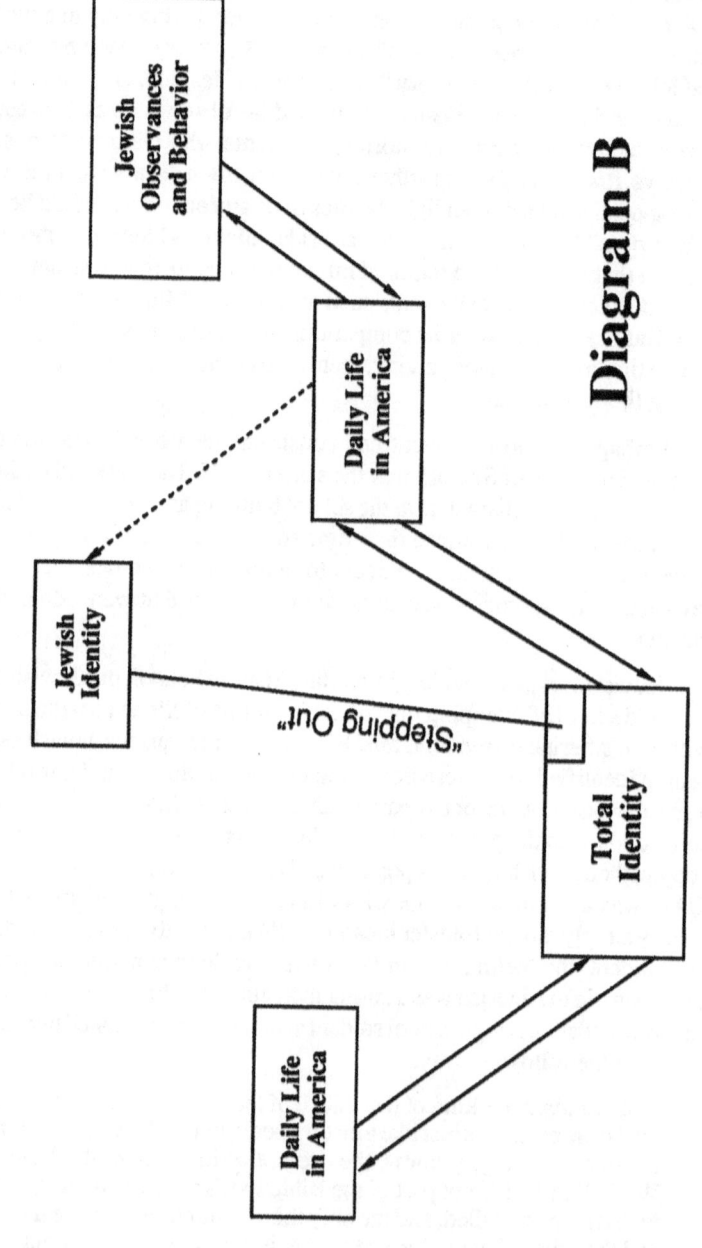

Jewish Identity — Attitudinal

The people of Shalom School perhaps found it easier to discuss Jewish identity in terms of behavior because of the considerable confusion, conflict, and sense of emptiness they felt regarding the relationship between their whole set of attitudes, values, and goals and their Jewish attitudinal identity. Many were not sure of their values and feelings. Some believed that they lived and thought according to certain Jewish standards but were unable to specify those standards. A number of people believed that Jewish and American values were one in the same, while others felt there was a strong conflict between what was perceived as Jewish and as American. Many people were simply unable to articulate any values or attitudes that seemed unique to the Jewish group. Finally, the largest number of people defined their Jewish attitudes and values in terms of what were not their values by rejecting the values of those who were not Jews (see Diagram C).

Non-Non-Jews

What stood out clearly as the most important factor in the Jewish identity of the people at Shalom School was the fact that they were not non-Jews. For some this was simply helpful as an identifying reference; but for many others it helped establish one's identity as a process of elimination, i.e. indicating what one was not; and, finally, for the remainder it indicated how one was superior to others in a highly chauvinistic sense.

In describing his Jewish identity, one parent used the non-non-Jewish theory exclusively to state his case. He said,

> Being Jewish is what you're not. It's what you don't believe in. You're not Christian, not Hindu, not Buddhist. You're not a Gentile so you're Jewish. What you're being taught in Hebrew school is that you're not a Gentile. But being Jewish doesn't entail believing in anything in particular.

This parent's thoughts closely resembled many students' comments on being Jewish. Many understood their Jewish identity as meaning only that they belonged to a different religion than other people. Typical of the students' comments was the following,

> Oh, it's just a different religion. We get presents on Hanukah; Christians get presents on Christmas.

Along these lines of the non-non-Jewish, Jewish identity were some who considered it positive to be different just for the sake of being different. One parent explained this to the researcher as follows:

> It's a sense of individuality. Especially around here where everybody is Christian. It doesn't matter what kind of Christian they are—Catholics, Protestants, just that they are Christians. And since you are not Christian—you are Jewish—it makes you unique.

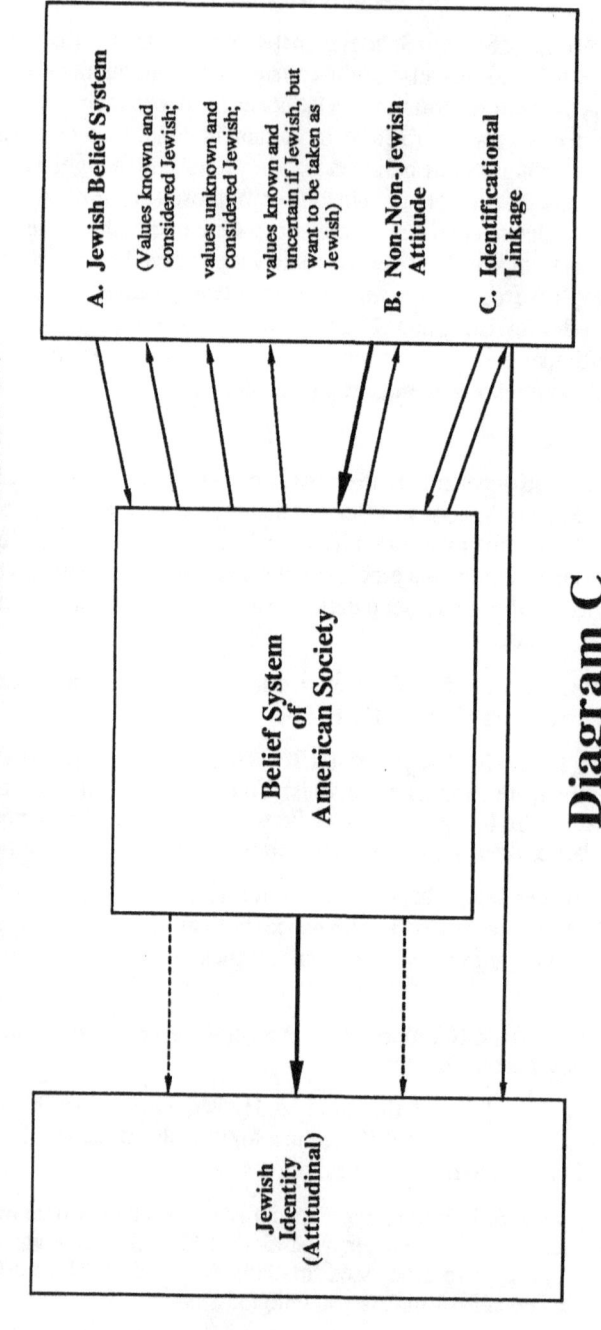

However, a number of the adherents to a non-non-Jewish, Jewish identity had a contempt for the non-Jew that accompanied a feeling of Jewish superiority and in so doing helped to identify elements of their Jewish identity. One teacher commented to the researcher that "If you knew me better you would know that I have a great respect for the Jewish people and little respect for all other people." The people that held this view saw the pattern of Jewish superiority extending over a wide range of topics. One mother covered a number of these topics, saying,

> I do know that Jewish families stand out in their dealing with children as being very different. The Jewish kids invite other kids over to their house to play. The Gentile kids in the class don't. The Jewish parents, both mother and father, go to all the meetings at school. The Gentile parents don't go much. The Jewish kids are more serious about their work - even if they goof off they have a sense of responsibility. There's more honesty, more requirements that kids live up to certain standards. And we've talked to a number of people about this and it seems to be fairly consistent. It really is true. The kids go to a Gentile house to play and it'll be time for lunch and they'll send the kids home. Now, in the Jewish house the kids will get fed.

Another parent spoke about the non-Jew during a discussion concerning her daughter and the possibility of inter-marriage. Unlike her husband she felt it was important for her daughter to marry another Jew. She said,

> I think it would be hard for her to marry out of her faith. Gentile husbands are different. It's a different kind of thing. Gentile husbands are different than Jewish husbands. I think a Jewish husband is more considerate of his wife.. He's always there when she needs him.

American Values and Jewish Values

One of the most important values of the parents of students in Shalom School, one which they did not consider to be a Jewish value, was material prosperity. The desire for material prosperity included the value of providing support for one's family in terms of food and shelter, but extended beyond that as well. There was a certain monetary standard of living that was expected from everyone and the social status of individuals within the community was judged at least in part, seemingly a very large part, by one's success in accumulating material wealth.

Although the value of material prosperity permeated every aspect of life among this group of people (see Schulweis 1978), it was never suggested that this value that was so primary in their lives, was in any sense a Jewish value. Rather, the value of material prosperity was linked by the Jews to the value system of the American capitalist system. As one teacher put it,

> These people have taken on the middle class culture of America. They have become super-materialists. They don't want to be doctors to practice medicine but to make money. It's just money for money's sake.

Another important value of the parents and teachers, this one frequently identified as a Jewish value, was the family. It was with fond memories that many of the parents spoke of growing up with grandparents and other members of an extended family close by. A Jewish person was said to be one who was always concerned for the welfare of members of one family and enjoyed close family ties. However, in the lives of the people of Shalom School, the tradition of the extended family had been abandoned.

Although there certainly was never any sign that children or the family as a whole were not loved or cared for, the great majority of parents and teachers in this community had left behind their extended family in another city to come to this location. While some had come for schooling and others for the scenery or climate, most people had moved away from family for economic reasons. Thus, while the family remained a Jewish value that these people believed in, it seemed to have become secondary in importance to the value of material prosperity. One mother, somewhat saddened but still clear about the changing priorities in her life, said:

> My grandmother gave us a sense of Jewish culture. My children have never seen their grandmother bake challah, bench licht[3], or make chicken soup. Never. There is a lack of people who are rich with Jewish cultural experience. There is a value in having people around with that experience and age. But this is where the work was. It was economics. And you have a different relationship when you live apart from family.

Another parent, a father, was less sentimental in discussing his choice to live in this town away from family. He said,

> We've chosen to live here. We're not living in Israel. It's convenient; it's comfortable. We enjoy living in suburbia despite the hardships [family]. We've chosen not to live in New York City.

Education is another value that has long been honored by the Jewish people. From the days of the Bible, Jews have been instructed to teach their children and to respect the learned man (and woman). But again, the "people of the book" seem to have adapted the value of education to coincide with the tradition of American capitalism that involved competing for material prosperity. Education has still retained its valued status but now its value is seen primarily in terms of of its economic rewards. Parents and children at Shalom School value their learning in terms of the professional monetary rewards that will come as a result of success in education. A good education, these people have learned through experience, will allow today's students to maintain or improve upon the normative material standards of the middle class in the future. Schulweis (1978:4) comments on the influence of middle class economic values in this regard, saying

> The acquisition of Jewish wisdom is to cultivate the heart, not to fatten the purse. Middle-classism has severed the drive from the moral goal... The

Jewish child is left with pressure without the nobility of a purpose which transcends the material and hedonistic gains.

As a result of this changing attitude toward education, not all schooling was valued equally. One graduate of Shalom School estimated the value of that school to the Jewish community in the following blunt manner: "Hebrew school doesn't matter." While some of the younger students could not articulate the distinction they made between what they called "regular school" and "Jewish school," some of the older students recognized and spoke of the difference in material terms. A seventh grade girl told the researcher,

> Public school is more important because you can go to college and stuff like that but this [Jewish school] you don't have to know to live or anything. Not everyone's gonna go to Israel, y'know. But you have to know math. I don't feel like this is much of a school—it's kind of a stupid place.

Finally, a parent, like so many others who made this material distinction in defining the value of education, said the following to the researcher, expressing her own views through her children's mouths:

> When they go to public school they see it as necessary for college or professional or business fields. But I don't feel they see it as essential that you be equipped with a Jewish background when you go out into the world.

Another value identified as being clearly Jewish was being undermined at least in part, by the routine of people's lives in America. This value, the ideal of the Jewish Sabbath, was under attack by the pressures of time and the structure of the American week and routine. Thus, this ideal of a day of rest, reflection, study, etc. was not diminished as an ideal but neither was it incorporated into people's lives. Students explained that Saturday was a day for cleaning and shopping, and that the local schools scheduled all their parties and dances on Friday night. One teacher told me, "I try to have a regular Sabbath dinner, but if there are other things to do I don't." Another teacher had to manage a restaurant on Friday night. A parent said he liked going to religious services on Friday evening (the researcher, however, did not find him in attendance on any of a number of observed evenings) stated that by going Friday he could "get it over with and have the weekend free." He explained that if he went Saturday morning "it wastes time that could be spent playing tennis or golf." Finally, another parent described her particular difficulty in maintaining a Sabbath observance:

> I try and remember to light the Shabbos candles, but with working, and subbing, and running, and doctor's appointments sometimes we forget. And sometimes we eat out on Friday night because the whole week has been exhausting.

Although they spoke in vague terms, many Jewish parents and teachers spoke about Jewish values in terms of a moral and ethical standard. It was not infrequent that in describing a good deed they had performed, people would attribute their attitude and action to a Jewish code. Typical of this was the following parent's glowing self-description, "At work I'm considered to be a righteous, moral, fair individual and I can only attribute that to my Jewish background." What were described in these moral codes were beliefs and values that were not unique to Judaism but were thought nonetheless to be part of Judaism. One parent described some of these values in the following way:

> The golden rule, cognizant of other's feelings, my freedom extends as far as you, dealing with other people honestly, fair—these are religious values but I picked them up as a Jew.

Others felt that Jewish and American values had so merged that it had become difficult to distinguish between them. People paused to think of the source of their values after they would at first automatically assert that the "Golden Rule" was their guiding standard. They wondered aloud as to whether this ideal was a Jewish, American or even universally held belief. Some parents rejected the idea of there being some unique Jewish values as being an "elitist" thought. One remarked emphatically that "there is one set of manners and attitudes." From a different reference point, another parent agreed that today there was one standard in America, but she argued that its source was Judaism. She said, "I know that Judaism teaches ethics, values, and morality—I'm not sure these haven't become American standards today." But there were still others, although fewer in number, who disagreed emphatically with this point of view. This second view felt that Jewish values and American values were in fact-to-face conflict. Although this perspective was more readily apparent to the teachers from Israel, one American teacher expressed the problem in the following manner:

> I don't believe institutions like synagogues embody the Jewish values or spirit... If synagogues ran on Jewish principles, I don't think it could survive. It [Judaism] doesn't go with the political, social, economic values of American life. It's not the way we grow up here. It's antithetical to our whole existence in this country."

Among many of the students there was an attitude that objected to the idea of there being any differences between Jew and non-Jew. They accepted the fact of their identification with a group other than that to which their non-Jewish friends identified, but they did not accept the fact that such an identification could have any affect on their personal identities. As one teacher stated,

> The kids know they're Jewish and are proud of it, but they really resent when other people try to make them different because they're Jewish.

Many Jews of Shalom School had little or no Jewish behavioral identity and had an empty and confused Jewish attitudinal identity. Nevertheless, these Jews felt strongly about being a part of the Jewish group regardless of the fact that many neither acted or thought in any particular or unique manner because they were

Jewish. These Jews, who identified but were otherwise without Jewish identity, were representative of the majority of people at Shalom School (see Diagram D). This disposition of the people of Shalom School reaffirms what Sklare and Greenblum (1967) discovered in their earlier study of a Jewish community, and shows that the problem, if anything, is not subsiding but perhaps increasing. Herman (1977:53) concludes that "the problem...is thus not so much one of identification with the Jewish group as of giving distinctiveness to their identity as Jews." It appears that the form that identity has taken is what Kelman (1977:22) warned about as the alternative "to the incorporation of Jewish identity into an authentic, integrated personal identity." That alternative, which is so descriptive of the people of Shalom School, he describes as:

> ...a Jewish identity that is offered in maximal form but accepted in minimal form—stripped of content, playing an insignificant role in the person's daily life or existential choices, and activated only when there is an opportunity for status enhancement or a threat to group survival.

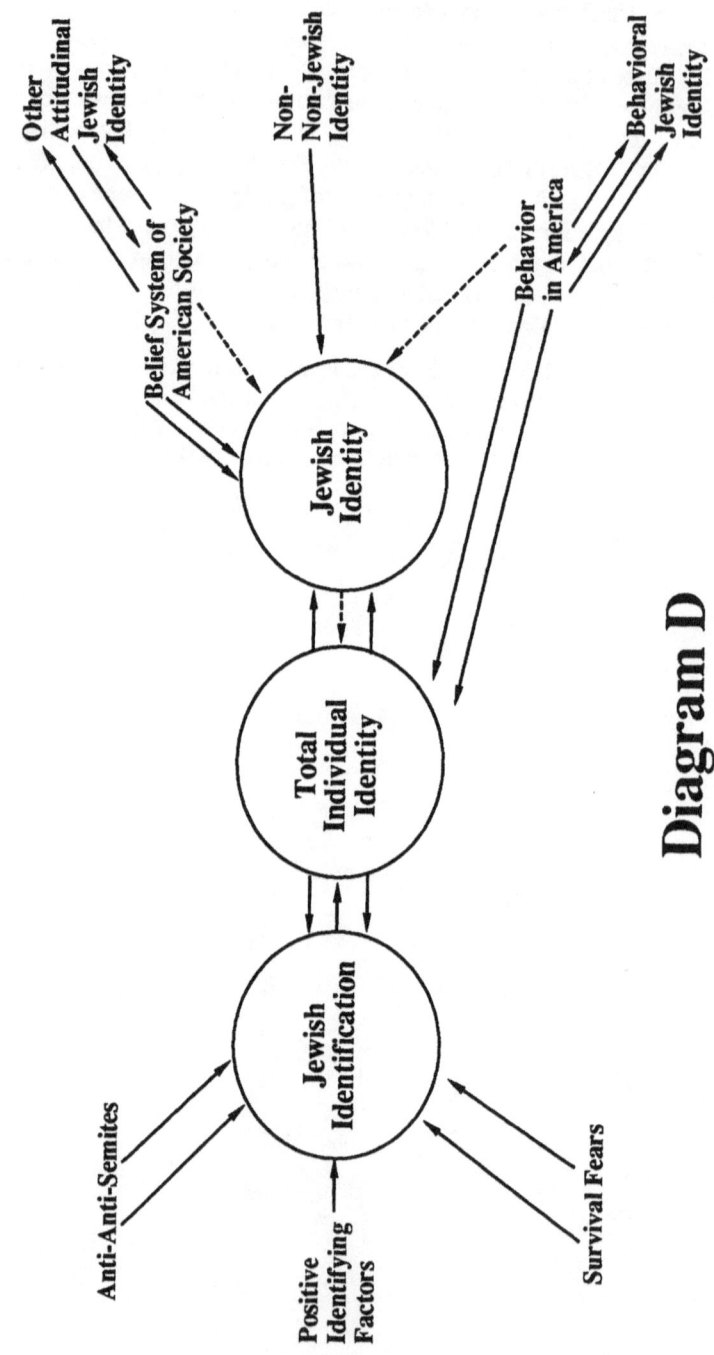

Chapter Four

SEARCHING FOR THE JEWISH COMMUNITY

There existed among the parents of Shalom School an acknowledgement that the Jewish community in which they lived represented something far different than they or their parents had grown up with. Whether this change was caused by modern transportation technology, new economic priorities, or a breakdown in traditional values was not their concern. Yet, in what seemed like a journey through unchartered waters, they found themselves in communities in which they were living, working, and socializing on a daily basis with people other than Jews. This was not a course necessarily undesired by the parents of Shalom School, yet for many it presented new challenges and new problems. As Jews, it brought to their very doorstep the conflicts of living as a minority in a pluralistic society. Furthermore, it appeared to create for the Jewish people a new and impersonal sense about their community whose reality they were as yet unwilling to confront.

The Neighborhood Community

Some parents of Shalom School continued to think of the Jewish community in terms of Jewish immigrant settlements in New York City at the turn of the twentieth century. For others the image was updated, but it still showed generations of families living together, with block after city block of tightly built homes filled only with Jews, with Jewish businesses lining the streets, Jewish children playing together, and fathers and sons walking together to the synagogue on Saturday morning. But the Jews of Shalom School did not live in these visions. They found themselves in a different time and in a very different world known as suburbia.

Spatial Separation

Apple River was one of the small suburban towns from which Jews came to Shalom School. In Apple River there were new, wide streets, and large homes surrounded by spacious grounds with garage space for two cars. There was little industry in the area and most of the people in this professional community commuted to work. People depended on their cars for transportation and it was only by car in about a fifteen minute drive that one could reach the Shalom Synagogue and Shalom School.

The matter of distance seemed to have had an important effect on people. It was a change to find that one's friends or one's children's friends rarely lived next door and often not within walking distance of one's home. Even one's neighbors, whether they were considered good friends or not, were spread a farther distance apart and were spatially separated in architectural terms, farther from one another than people could remember it being in their own childhood. Distance from the synagogue and school served as a barrier to those who could remember living within walking distance of the synagogue as a child. As one parent said, "Because of distances—suburbia—it is almost impossible to get to school and synagogue as frequently. The closeness is missing." Another father expressed a similar sentiment saying that the physical outlay of suburbia was an impediment to Jewish observance. He said,

> I'm lazy. I would like to do more religious things, be more Jewish, more active, help out. But living in suburbia, it's an inconvenience. So if you're not totally committed you're going to find excuses not to do things. But I enjoy religion, the services, Judaism, and yet I don't go nearly as often as I'd like.

The impact of distance on observance was felt strongly by an Israeli teacher who had only recently come to the United States. Familiar with a spatially close Jewish community where she lived in Israel, she found herself facing new problems when she realized she could not attend synagogue services without driving to them. Although she was not a religious Jew and did not object to driving on religious grounds, she described to the researcher the crisis she felt during the Yom Kippur holiday:

> In Israel, you don't have to act being a Jew. But here, I had to drive to synagogue and I felt: 'if I have to drive I'm not going to fast.' And I felt terrible about it. Here you have to emphasize everything seven times as much.

Integration with Non-Jews

Besides the fact that homes in the neighborhood were set a distance apart from one another, the homes in Apple River were also frequently not filled with Jewish families. One parent, Mrs. Sidney, related a story she had heard from a new home-buyer in the neighborhood pointing to the scarcity yet noteworthiness of Jews living in the area. While driving down her street, the real-estate agent, a person unknown to the Sidney's, told the prospective buyer, "there is the home of the Sidney's, the other Jewish family in the area." Mrs. Sidney's shocked reaction to this story was a feeling that she must be known to her neighbors as "Sidney, the Jewish family."

For many families, the feeling of isolation as Jews in Apple River made them recall a rosy picture of "the way it used to be." One mother expressed her difficulty in adjusting to Apple River. She said,

> Since I moved here I have had to fight hard not to assimilate and not to lose my identity. Back in _____, it was much easier. There were friends and family and neighbors and grandparents. And this was supposed to be a big Jewish area, but I have very few Jewish friends.

The children of Shalom School had the same problem as their parents meeting Jewish friends, but they did not have memories of life ever being any different. It was common for the students of Shalom School to attend public schools in which there was only a handful of other Jews in the entire school. To counter this problem, parents encouraged their children and hoped that through their attendance at Shalom School Jewish friendships might develop. But, again, the matter of distance interfered in the development of these friendships. One student explained that her difficult in making Jewish friends was because "I live kind of far away from some of the kids and I don't really know them that well." Another parent commented: "The things my kids aren't getting—well, when I was growing up my grandparents lived with us. We spoke Yiddish at home. My kids don't even have Jewish neighbors or a Jewish neighborhood."

Choosing Suburbia

Despite the many fond memories of the Jewish community of their childhood, the parents of Shalom School had moved to suburbia as a matter of choice. While they wished to be within driving distance of a synagogue, their choice of neighborhood was based primarily on socio-economic considerations. They were interested in living in the biggest house in the wealthiest neighborhood they could afford, regardless of the ethnicity of the community. As one parent active in the school said, "I don't want to live in a Jewish community but I do want to maintain a Jewish milieu." The feelings of another parent were that he had become more observant precisely because of the lack of a spatially tight-knit Jewish community. "When I grew up," he said, "we celebrated Christmas more than Hanukah. But we lived in a Jewish neighborhood. But it's better here—they [the children] have a better view of Catholicism and other people."

The Changing Family

Another change that was more evident among congregants of the reform temple in the town than among the Shalom Synagogue residents was in the family structure. While the researcher encountered only a few cases of "joined" families[4] and interfaith marriages, and no cases of single-parent families, it was estimated that the membership of the nearby reform temple was comprised of 25-50% single-parent and "joined" families. The non-typical types of families interviewed at the Shalom School all indicated that they were subjected to special problems in the Jewish community either due to resistance from other Shalom Synagogue members or from pressures from divorced spouses. Perhaps also due to the changing relationships of marriage partners and the trend toward equalization of male and female roles, the researcher found a number of instances in which one member of a couple openly resisted or withdrew from responsibility for Jewish observance in the home or the Jewish education of the children.

The Business Community

Parents also had memories of growing up in a neighborhood in which the Jewish butcher shop was located down the street from the Jewish bakery which was three doors down from the Jewish book and gift shop. Located in-between these stores were Jewish neighbors and friends who owned various retail stores. Today, the few Jewish residents of Apple River who still wanted to shop from the Jewish butcher or bakery or bookstore had to travel in different directions for at least thirty minutes to find one of each. Sometimes the local supermarkets or speciality ethnic food stores carried a few Jewish products, and the synagogue did operate a very small gift shop at irregular hours, but the feeling was not the same. The language, the discussions, the smells, and the faces were different.

Spatial Separation

Another change was the practice of commuting to work. Each morning, en masse, the men and sometimes women, too, left Apple River in their automobiles headed primarily towards the greater metropolitan center. If there was a sense that Apple River was a Jewish community, for the overwhelming majority the sense of the environment of the workplace was certainly not Jewish. Again, the distance and the new business environments were elements that the parents of Shalom School felt were working against their Jewishness. As another parent stated, "It's very hard to observe the Jewish religion because it's made for you to live within four blocks of the synagogue and work within two blocks..."

Integration with Non-Jews

Some parents, although few in number, either perceived or had actually experienced anti-semitism in the non-Jewish workplace. One working mother described the troubling effect that being a Jew in the non-Jewish workplace had had on her:

> I have been looking for a teaching job for four years. I never bring out in an interview the fact that I am Jewish. If I am asked, it is a different story. I am not ashamed to be a Jew, but I am really aware of a lot of anti-semitism; and there is so much prejudice around. When I was asked about my volunteer work I answered that I worked for a non-philanthropic organization. I would not say I have worked for Bnai Brith women. I didn't want it to hamper my chances. I thought that was a shame, but you have to be realistic. Especially as a substitute teacher—if I was bad, the kids would say, 'What a bad Jewish teacher.'

Many of the students, whose workplace was the public school, had also experienced uncomfortable feelings, if not anti-semitism, in their relations with non-Jews. As was mentioned earlier, it was typical for students to have fewer than two or three Jewish classmates at their public schools. An example of the type of situations students objected to was described by a seventh grade girl:

In school, during Christmas in art, everyone is making Christmas cards. And the teacher goes, 'If anyone doesn't want to do these because of their religion raise your hand.' That was really dumb. I knew I was going to be the only one to raise my hand and I didn't want to. And so after everyone sat down I went to him and said, 'I don't want to do this because I don't celebrate Christmas.' And he said, 'Why didn't you raise your hand?' And I just didn't want to—it's kind of embarrassing. And he said, 'What religion are you?' And I didn't think that was any of his business, but I said, 'I'm Jewish.' And he goes, 'Y'know, you look Jewish.' And I couldn't believe he said that—I thought he had...I was just cracking up. That was so dumb.

The public school affected Jewish life in another, but different way. School activities, particularly social activities, were regularly scheduled on Friday evening which for a family attempting to observe the Jewish Sabbath could only cause conflict. One mother explained to the researcher the difficulty she and her family experienced trying to have Friday dinners together and sometimes with company. She said,

> But this is very difficult. In the community, Friday night is the big night. We are constantly fighting the calendar because they [the school] are constantly putting a big event on Friday night—dances, parties, open house.

The contrast between public school and the all-Jewish Shalom School helped the students recognize the special tensions and pressures they felt as Jews at public school. One girl said with an expression of relief that she enjoyed being with Jewish friends "because when you're talking everyone knows what you're talking about; you don't have to explain." Similarly, a sixth grade boy described why he felt so much more comfortable at Shalom School than his public school:

> You can tell Christian jokes without getting in trouble. At public school you can get sent to the principal and get expelled. It's really tight. Well, they tell jokes about us and they don't get into trouble. Here [Shalom School] everyone knows you're Jewish. You don't have to worry about anyone calling you a 'creep' or anything because you can call them right back and it'll just be the same.

Choosing Suburbia

Despite these feelings of being uncomfortable and at times isolated as a Jew, there was no movement and little interest in reversing the trend of full integration into the non-Jewish community. As one mother stated,

> There is a tinge of isolation that goes on in an isolated community and I don't know what to do about it. I can't transplant New York here. I can't put my children in an all Jewish school except to take them out of the community.

Because the people of Shalom School did not think of themselves in terms of being Jewish during their daily routine, these problems as Jews, however real, were not constantly weighing on their minds. It is more accurate to depict the Jews of Shalom School as being happy and comfortable in their chosen Apple River community. Only in matters that were of lesser importance, such as their Jewishness, did they have to make certain compromises which although they regretted, they were still willing to live with. Nevertheless, these compromises were building to make for a new definition of the Jewish community for the Jews of Shalom School.

The Spiritual Jewish Community

The suburban Jewish community had a different design than the urban and ghetto Jewish communities prior to it in that it was highly integrated into the non-Jewish community and world. Nevertheless, a Jewish community did exist, although it was less personal, more divided, more bureaucratic and structured, and based heavily on survival fears.

The structure of the Jewish family had changed from one that was extended to one that was nuclear and even that was showing strong signs of changing even further. Although parents saw to it that their children attend the Jewish afternoon school, they did not feel or attempt to take any personal responsibility for their children's education. Observances as a Jewish family continued, but for the majority it was in a minimal and irregular fashion. Special rituals such as Bar/Bat Mitzvah, marriage, and burial were, significantly, still upheld. However, an interest in things "American" and the pressures and demands that accompanied that interest predominated activity and thought in the family.

Friendships with Jews and Non-Jews

Many of the parents indicated that although it was sometimes difficult, they still maintained many close Jewish friendships. Their desire for friendships with other Jews came from feeling more comfortable among Jews than among non-Jews, as one mother stated, "I feel more comfortable among Jews—sometimes someone throws in a Jewish word. We're different." However, the relationship in most of these Jewish friendships did not develop or include things Jewish. Rather, they are best described as being friendships with other Jews who wanted to share, grow, and do things American.

The children, who had less independent mobility in their environment, were less able to meet other Jewish children because of the very small numbers of Jews present in the various neighborhood public schools they attended. Many parents looked to the Jewish school as a primary source for Jewish social contact for their children. One mother said, "I send my kids [to Shalom School] because they can't be Jewish by themselves. They need other Jews around them." Yet the limited amount of time at Shalom School presented difficulties for friendship building, as another parent remarked, "It is hard for kids to make friends in Hebrew school when they don't see them but two times a week." It was also difficult for children from the few highly observant families not to feel isolated. Without the support of an extended family or a close peer group who lived and observed in a similar fashion, confusion and resentment sometimes surfaced. One such seventh grade student explained this problem in her own words:

> I have to go to services on Saturday but I don't like it. I'd rather stay home and watch T.V. Sometimes I like the Friday night meal because we all eat together and the rest of the week we don't. But I don't feel good about being Jewish because none of my friends are, and it's hard because I can't do anything on Saturday; especially because other Jewish kids do stuff on Saturday and my friends can't understand. You can't explain everything!

Importing Jewish Models

Over half of the Shalom School staff lived outside the imaginary but perceived Shalom Synagogue membership boundaries. It was the principal's intention in hiring staff to choose individuals who could serve as Jewish role models for their students. Some parents indicated that they would have liked the staff to be visible outside of school hours so their children could see them "practice what they preach." Nevertheless, these people were not members of the synagogue nor were they considered part of the community. Although the staff was given responsibility for teaching the children of the community about the heritage of the Jewish people, there was no attempt made to bring these teachers into the community. Rather, what developed between the staff and parents over the course of the year was an ever-widening gap. One teacher, who attempted to become more a part of the community by attending synagogue services on three occasions early in the year, reported that no one even came up to her to say hello. She added,

> There was a sense of my being strange or not quite on their level. I was still just a college student in their eyes, not a professional. I think I'm a professional.

Two Israeli teachers, who had just come to the United States prior to the beginning of the school year, were also never welcomed or made to feel comfortable by the parents of the Shalom School, As a result of bad feelings increasing through the course of the year, one of the then hardened Israeli teachers told the researcher, "I wouldn't want to be a part of the community. I want to finish my studies and go home."

Affiliation, not Friendship

Apparently, the attitude of not making new teachers feel more comfortable extended to new synagogue members as well. One parent, who since his arrival had taken a leadership position in one of the synagogue organizations, angrily recalled his bitter feelings when his family had first moved to Apple River:

> It really angered me when they were teaching [at Shalom School] Johnny [his son, 2nd grade] about Tzedakah.[5] And I felt very annoyed. Because when we arrived we didn't feel any from anyone...I don't know why we went to the Temple in the first place, but we wanted to live near Jews. It's a Jewish thing to help one another and they didn't want to help us. They talked to us but without any personal feeling or interest.

Other parents, too, who were active in the synagogue and held leadership positions, indicated that the synagogue did not provide a community for them. Those less involved in synagogue activities indicated to the researcher that to them either the synagogue stood for religion and not for community, or that they were not comfortable in the synagogue, or simply that they were not interested. As one parent stated,

> I don't look to the Temple to spend more of my time. I don't have a need for it. I only go because I like the Rabbi.

Many of the parents of Shalom School, in addition to holding membership in the synagogue and in its various organizations, were members or supporters of an assortment of other Jewish groups. Among these groups were the Jewish Welfare Federation, Hadassah, Israel Bonds, United Synagogue, etc. Indeed, Gordon's analysis (1964) of the Jewish experience in America was that despite their having been culturally assimilated to a substantial degree, their strong independent structural network had accounted for their survival as an ethnic group. Nevertheless, at least within the structure of the synagogue, a protective attitude towards its own individual organization sometimes interfered and even undermined the overall goals, however undefined, of the entire synagogue. One exasperated congregational board member explained his frustrations:

> There it is—the congregation, Sisterhood, Men's Club—and we're all working for the same goal. And they fight among themselves over such petty things. Sisterhood fights Men's Club, this one fights that one. And why do they waste their time—they're all giving money to the same place!? They just wash it away with all their pettiness. Many people on the congregation board don't join the Men's Club. They purposely don't belong! They don't want to support the organization that's supporting the congregation.

Many Jews of Shalom School supported Israel emotionally, financially, and organizationally. Contact with Israeli groups, trips to Israel, and support of Israeli organizations were strongly encouraged. Yet relations between individual American and Israeli Jews was mixed, at the very best. One parent commented, "I think Americans and Israelis have to re-examine their relationship because now both groups are just using one another without accepting each other.

At the Shalom School there was antagonism from the staff towards the organizations that were in positions to support the school. The Jewish Community Center in whose building the school was housed was considered uncooperative, even hostile at times, toward the school. The Bureau of Jewish Education, supported by and intended to benefit Jewish education in the entire metropolitan area and its environs, was the subject of mockery and disdain from the principal and rabbi. Similarly, the educational network of the Conservative Movement to which the synagogue and school belonged was considered to be of little or no benefit. In addition, there was an added feeling of resentment since these various groups were perceived to be so well-funded while the school staff and school board considered themselves financially strapped.

Attempts at "Renewal"

As a response to something lacking either in the family, or the community, or both, a new type of communal group was begun among people from Shalom Synagogue. Called a "Havurah" (meaning collective, or group of friends), it was comprised of approximately five to nine families. Since the first group had started without formal synagogue input about three years earlier, another eleven groups had been organized with seven still active. Although there was a precedent for the Havurah in other Jewish cities and suburbs throughout the U.S., the Shalom Synagogue Havurot (plural) operated entirely independently, establishing all goals, responsibilities, and commitments according to each group's wishes. In general most of the groups met only once per month for social events or discussions. Some of the groups met one night during the holiday of Passover for the traditional Seder.

Despite the high goals associated with the Havurah, the predominant reason individual parents gave for joining a Havurah was "so my children can have a Jewish contact." For themselves, the parents saw the Havurah as a casual, unimportant gathering which was too often devoted to planning the following month's activity. One parent said she was "wary about people she didn't know in the group", another said that he now realized he didn't miss the extended family anyway, and others complained about one or two particularly elitist Havurot that contained all the synagogue leaders. The children were generally positive about the Havurot, although one student's comments substantiated the casual commitment ascribed to them. He said,

> Not that greaat. Everyone goes off their own way. Everyone says they're going for ice cream and two families take off home. You know what I mean?

A recurring comment concerning involvement in the Jewish community was that people were participating for the benefit of others. Parents of Shalom School frequently noted to the researcher that whether it be attending synagogue services, joining a Havurah, or lighting Friday night candles, their reason for doing so was either to please their own folks or to provide for their children but their reason was not to do it for themselves. The children often stated that when their participation at Shalom School or other Jewish activities was not based on parental coercion, it was done so as to please their parents and grandparents. Finally, the staff indicated that their primary motive for education and sometimes community participation was for the sake of the children and the parents of Shalom School.

A Summation: The External Jewish Community

Their children attended the Jewish school and would have the Bar/Bat Mitzvah. It was anticipated by the parents of the Shalom School that weddings would be performed by a rabbi in the synagogue and burials would take place in the Jewish cemetery. Sometimes the family lit Sabbath candles on Friday night. The parents were members of the synagogue, the wife belonged to Hadassah, the husband to the Men's Club, and both strongly supported the politics of whatever party was in power in Israel. They carefully read about Israel and stories of anti-semitism in the newspapers. They were confident that Jewish organizations and lobbies would be representing them and working diligently for the proper Jewish concerns. They would attend synagogue services on Rosh Hashanah and when they were invited to Bar/Bat Mitzvahs. Their own parents would fly into town periodically, and sometimes the visit would coincide with a Jewish holiday. Many of their social friends were Jewish.

The parents of the Shalom School had a deep concern for Jewish survival. However, their involvement in things Jewish outside of survival fears was done for the sake of others. Their days were consumed by the non-Jewish people, events, businesses, and neighborhoods in which they lived. They may have belonged to a Jewish organization but they expected the organization to do the work, not themselves. If they did get involved, they were often dissatisfied and unhappy with others around them. They supported Israel but preferred not to have anything to do with Israelis. They had Jewish friends but they didn't do anything Jewish with them. They could recall with good memories that things were different when they were young, but they were content to keep those memories in the past. Those few who wished to be more observant were even further isolated and had a very difficult time finding more than a handful of others like themselves. The children even found it hard to locate other children who were Jewish unless special arrangements were made.

Sometimes these people did think of themselves as part of the Jewish community, but they did so primarily when the question of survival was at stake. Those who were more observant may have shared in the community more often knowing that other Jews were doing as they did around the world, but they were in the minority. Also, those who belonged and were active in organizations felt somewhat closer to the community when it was their organization that they read about. In addition, there did, in a sense, exist a local Jewish community, just as there was a metropolitan Jewish community, a national Jewish community, and a world Jewish community.

Although the people of Apple River felt a commitment to a Jewish community, it was, however, not to one that was personal, or in an immediate sense, "their" community. The Jewish community was no longer made up of Jesse, Davida, Mark, or Esther; rather, it was a Jewish community that was nameless and faceless and without sufficient human warmth. To them the Jewish community was not their family, not the neighbor next door, not even the synagogue or the Jewish school. It was most often what they read about in books. It was comprised of large, bureaucratic organizations whose leaders spoke "on behalf" of the Jewish community. In some ways it was almost mythical. Certainly it was distant and impersonal. Just as these people had to "step out" of their daily lives to be Jewish, so it was that for them the Jewish community had come to exist "outside" of themselves, external to the very people who comprised it and for whom it was meant to stand.

PART III
INSIDE THE JEWISH AFTERNOON SCHOOL

Chapter Five

ARRIVING AT SHALOM SCHOOL: WHY ARE WE HERE

The Decision to Affiliate and Attend

Association with Shalom School, although not a significant element in the total lives of the majority of the people who had some connection with it, was indeed a significant factor in their lives as Jews. For most people the school was the only Jewish event in their lives that they felt committed to observe not only weekly, but two or three times each week, even if for parents this meant only responsibility for transportation and listening to complaints.

The "Ritual" of Affiliation

In explaining their reason for sending their children to Shalom School, parents recurringly alluded to their decision in terms of ritual (Schoem 1982). A member of the school board told the researcher that she sent her children because "everybody else did it—I'll do it, too. The grandparents expect you to do it and the parents expect you to do it." A teacher explained that sending one's child to a Jewish school was "a way of life—just like sending kids to college." The students, too, were keenly aware of this "automatic response" to Jewish schooling. Although most students indicated that they were unwillingly forced to attend Shalom School, they clearly recognized that they would be sending their own children to Jewish school when they grew older. As one ten-year old boy put it, "If we get it, they get it!"

Linked closely to the ritual of attendance at Jewish school was the even more widely adhered-to ritual of the Bar/Bat Mitzvah. In fact, the term "Bar/Bat Mitzvah factory" was used frequently by staff members to describe the Jewish school. A very influential member of the school board explained her understanding of the relation of the school to the Bar/Bat Mitzvah. She said:

> Hebrew school is a boring thing. Why should we have to entertain the kids. The goal is the Bar Mitzvah. And when they stand on the Bimah (pulpit) you don't want to embarrass you or themselves. Okay? That's where it really is.

Parents believed that the realization of one's identification with the Jewish people came through the ritual of attendance at the Jewish school, culminating in the ritual ceremony of the Bar/Bat Mitzvah. It was the performance of the ritual, much more than any evaluation of its content, that was of importance to the majority of parents. Indeed, most parents didn't even want to face questions about the quality of the school. Although they realized that their children were unhappy there and some listened to their children's complaints, their overriding concern was simply to be sure that their children were in attendance and that the school was operated on schedule and in an orderly fashion. One parent expressed this attitude, saying:

> The kids really don't like Hebrew school, but that may even be traditional. You know, on occasion, Eddie has told me he hates Hebrew school, and I say, 'Edward, that's wonderful. You're carrying on a Jewish tradition. Because when I went to Hebrew school I hated it, too. Because all good Jews hate Hebrew school.

Fulfilling Responsibility

It appeared, as well, that some parents used their children's attendance at the school as a means of reasserting their own Jewish identification and of establishing their own Jewish behavioral identity. Although it was a very detached medium for behavior, as the parents viewed their responsibility largely as paying tuition, providing transportation, and listening to complaints, it nevertheless fulfilled in their minds the Biblical responsibility of "teach it to your children." It was also important because it was a recurring behavior, in that it occurred at least twice weekly, even though it was clearly the children who had to bear the greatest share of that burden. Still other parents, who were desirous of becoming more involved and educated Jewishly, looked to their children's schooling in the hope that the children, in turn, would teach the parents more about being Jewish.

Jewish Identification and Jewish Identity

Once their children were in the school, the parents began to build expectations for the school program. Foremost among these was the development of Jewish identification. In this context, the parents thought about identification in terms of their children learning to distinguish themselves as non non-Jews and developing a "good feeling" about being Jewish. As part of the identification expectation, and because of the great changes they perceived in Jewish community life, parents placed a great value on the development of a Jewish group for their children. It was their fervent hope that the few hours per week of social contact with Jews at Shalom School could be an adequate substitute for what was lacking in Jewish community in their public schools and neighborhoods. Also of some importance to the parents and seen as the traditional method for building identification and identity was the gaining of knowledge of the Jewish heritage through the study of history, Hebrew, Bible, Israel, and the prayer book.

There was a small but vocal group of parents, comprised of those who either were more behaviorally observant of Jewish laws, traditions, and customs or perceived themselves to be so, who expected the Jewish school to conduct itself on a different basis. They expected the school to teach their children about a Jewish "Way of Life"—one in which every thought and practice were founded in traditional

Jewish terms. They expected the school to present an image to their children that this was not only how Jews had lived in the past but it represented how Jews were living in the present, even in their own community. The clear implication was that the students could, should, and perhaps already were living that way. This group of parents, however, did not realize the flagrant inconsistency of their own lives with their own expectations for the school. Furthermore, although these parents wanted the school to project a Jewish "Way of Life" image to their children, it was clearly not their intention that their children live up to that image once outside of the school walls.

Staff members associated with the school for a number of reasons. Out of personal consideration, some staff members chose to work in the Jewish school as a means of establishing ties with a Jewish institution and community, and/or like the parents, of re-asserting for themselves their identification with the Jewish people and things Jewish. Other staff members accepted their positions from an already established commitment and love for things Jewish, hoping that by sharing their personal good feelings from Judaism they could influence young Jewish students in a similar way. An equally important consideration on the part of staff members was their attraction to the salary offer. As a part-time position, the pay was considered excellent by the largely non-professionally certified staff.

It was the expectation of members of the school staff that parents and students would have rather strong Jewish identities and would be more than mildly interested in Jewish education. It was their hope that they could interest the students and parents to do more and think more as Jews, to become more interested in Israel, and to teach the students a core of knowledge in the areas of Bible, history, and Hebrew. Just like the previously described small group of parents, the rabbi and principal developed the curriculum and the teachers conducted their classes with the implicit understanding that underlying what was learned in the classroom was a Jewish "Way of Life" to which that learning could be used, experienced, developed, and enriched. The staff approached classroom instruction with the full yet self-deceptive belief that they, in their own lives, embodied this Jewish "Way of Life." As discussed earlier, however, this in truth, was simply not the case.

The students did not have a choice in their attendance at Shalom School prior to their Bar/Bat Mitzvah. The decision for them to attend was made by their parents. However, most students did have an opinion about their attendance. What some students liked about attending Shalom School was that in doing so they were pleasing their parents and grandparents. They also looked forward to enjoying the friendships they had developed at the school. Most students, even those who found things they liked about the school, told the researcher that given the choice, they would choose not to attend. As one of the seemingly happier students at Shalom School stated emphatically, "If I had a choice, I would say NO! ABSOLUTELY NOT!"

Most students understood the reason for their forced attendance at Shalom School as being training for their Bar/Bat Mitzvah. Other stated reasons were also related to identification or merely to the fact that it was a ritual to attend or "because everyone else goes." One girl said her purpose at school was "to learn about Jews so I can teach my children and grandchildren." Others understood that Shalom School was a place to meet Jewish friends and "know your religion." Still others had little idea as to why they were there. One unhappy boy stated, "Heck, if I know."

Although many Jews had to "step out" of their lives to do things Jewish and often found their Jewish community to be external to themselves, they still turned to the Jewish school as an important place to "be Jewish" and to build Jewish community, at least for the children. Perhaps it was even because of their awareness of the growing problems for themselves as Jews and for Jewish community life that prompted them to hold on to Jewish schooling as a significant element in their Jewish identification. Nevertheless, even as the school provided an important focus for these problems, what occurred at the school was more a reflection of those problems than a ready source of easy solutions.

A Technical Description of the School

The Jewish afternoon school under study was located in a suburb of 50,000 people outside a large metropolitan area with a population numbering over three million. This larger metropolitan population was counted among the top twenty population centers for Jews in North America. The area was noted for its ethnic diversity, wide-ranging cultural offerings, good transportation network, brilliant scenery, and temperate climate. Families who were associated with the school lived in a number of surrounding suburban cites with a range of approximately ten miles.

Facilities and Meeting Times

The school itself, comprised of about two hundred students, was housed in three separate locations. Children in K-3 studied in a local elementary school building, students in grades 8-12 came to a building located on the synagogue grounds, and students in grades 4-7 studied at the synagogue property as well as at a building belonging to the Jewish Community Center. It was about a five minute drive from the Jewish Community Center building to the synagogue property. It took approximately fifteen minutes by car to go from the Jewish Community Center to the elementary school building.

The three school locations were almost never used simultaneously. The students in grades K-3 attended school on Sunday mornings only from 9:30-12 Noon. All students in grades 4-7 attended on Sundays from 9:45-12:15 and on Wednesdays from 4-5:30 PM. Some of these students also attended school on Monday afternoons from 4-5:30. Students in grades 8-12 attended school on

Arriving at Shalom School: Why Are We Here

Monday evenings only, from 7:30-9:00 PM. Finally, a program called "Parent Education" was held at the synagogue property on Sundays from 10-11:30 AM on a very infrequent basis.

Meeting Time and Place

	Elementary School	Synagogue	Jewish Community Center
Sunday Morning	K-3	"Parent Ed"	4-7
Monday Afternoon		4-7	
Monday Evening		8-12	
Wednesday Afternoon			4-7

The public elementary school was used for classes because of its size, location, and cost. The section of the school that was used on Sunday morning was a one-story concrete structure. The rooms were rectangular in shape, decorated according to the design of the daily public school teacher. Half the rooms opened onto a concrete play area; the other rooms had access to a playground area.

The synagogue had two buildings (see Diagram E). The larger, primary structure was used for religious services, social events, large meetings, etc. On a hill behind this building lay a converted house which was used for classes. The rabbi's office, the combined synagogue/school office, a school supply room, and a library were also housed in this building. Classes were also held in the converted garage belonging to the house. The rooms were irregular in shape and size, some filled with long tables and folding chairs and others with desk chairs. There were few decorations on the wall. Immediately surrounding the synagogue property were two churches, a single house, and some undeveloped hillside land.

Classes for grades four through seven were held at the Jewish Community Center (see Diagram F). In addition to housing the school, the Center sponsored its own activities and programs and did not allow the school to decorate any of the rooms it used. Neither were the rooms furnished with classes in mind. One room had sofa lounging furniture, another a pool table, a third was in a very large social hall with very poor acoustics. Classes meeting on the floor below the social hall could hear all footsteps and any movements of desks and chairs from above. The school principal did not have a permanent office at this location, only an unused room available during school hours. There was a large dirt lot behind the building that the students used during recess. The Center was located in the midst of numerous apartment complexes.

Synagogue Oversight

Family membership in the synagogue, at a cost of several hundreds of dollars in dues was a prerequisite for attendance at the school. In addition, there was a charge for each student attending the school.

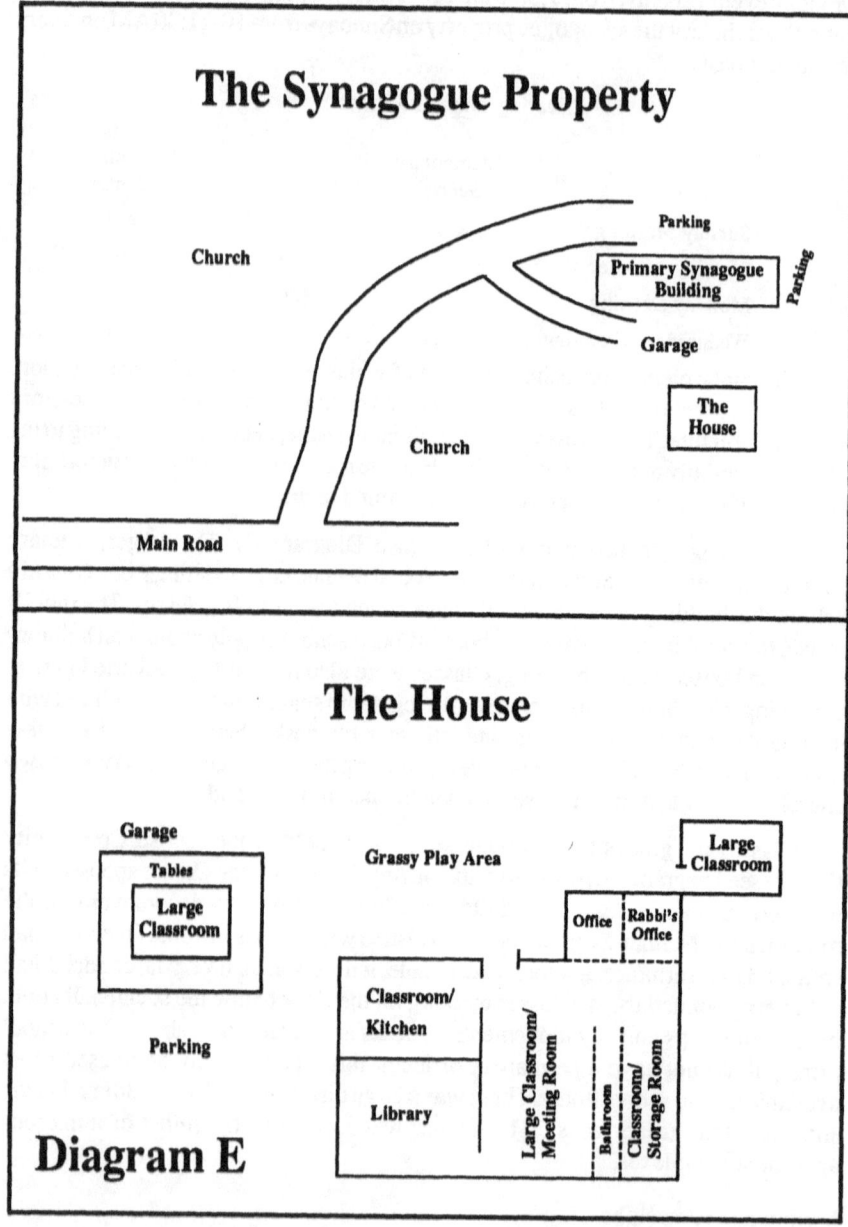

The Jewish Community Center Property

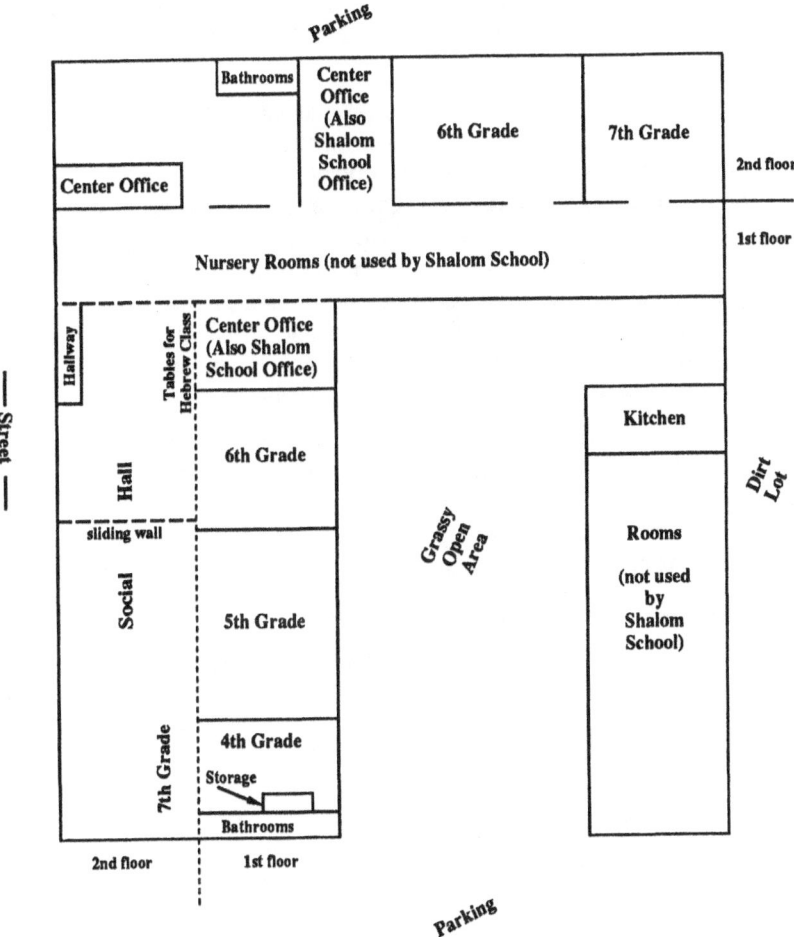

Diagram F

The synagogue membership each year elected a set of officers to oversee synagogue affairs. A board of about eighteen, including officers, directors, and men's club and sisterhood representatives, met monthly to discuss a wide variety of issues related to the synagogue. Topics ranged from budget to landscaping, and from Kashruth in the synagogue kitchen to education. Each year the synagogue board had to give final approval to the proposed school budget. The chairperson of the school board sat on the synagogue board.

The school board was comprised of approximately eight active (attended more than one meeting per year) members, almost all of whom were mothers of children in the school. Two fathers were listed as official members of the board; however, they never attended any meetings. The rabbi, a male, and the principal, a female, also attended these monthly board meetings. The school board was responsible for the hiring of the school principal and the planning of the school budget, both subject to the approval of the synagogue board. At meetings, this group discussed a wide range of topics related to the school such as fund raising, discipline problems, teacher problems, and parent complaints. The chairperson of the school board came to the school premises each session to help oversee activities.

The rabbi of the synagogue was actively involved with the school. In addition to teaching the pre-Bar/Bat Mitzvah students and some high school students he participated in curriculum development, policy planning, and the hiring of the staff. His opinion was frequently called upon for both small and large matters regarding the school. The rabbi had been at the synagogue for several years.

Administration and Organization

The principal, who had been at the school in this capacity for approximately five years, was employed half-time. At the end of the school year, her contract was renewed as a full-time position. The principal was immediately responsible for carrying out all of the policies, curricula, etc. that she, in conjunction with the rabbi, had developed, and which had met final approval from the school and synagogue boards. The principal was also responsible for all of the education programs in the synagogue, from pre-K to parent education. In addition to the principal, one teacher was assigned extra duties as an administrative assistant. This person had been the principal of the school several years earlier when the school population had been much smaller.

There were approximately fifteen part-time teachers in the school. Grades pre-K-5 were assigned one teacher each. The sixth and seventh grades, which were each divided into two classes, had one teacher for each class. The high school program had four teachers who were assigned by topic, not by grade. Five teachers worked in the optional enrichment program on Monday afternoons. Finally, a special tutor was available on Sundays for students in grades pre-K-7. Teachers were paid approximately seven to nine dollars per hour of instruction. Aides were paid a nominal amount as a token gesture. Teachers were also expected to attend monthly staff meetings.

Unlike the day schools that all of these students attended prior to the Jewish school, attendance at the afternoon school was not compulsory by state law. Therefore, it was the parents who saw to it that their children attended. The parents were invited to participate in the school structure either as school board members or as room mothers. There were a number of parents with children in the school who were also teachers in the school. Parents were also able to contact the principal, rabbi, teachers, or school board members to give input.

The students had no formal mechanism of input in the school. However, they were expected to attend all classes and behave in an appropriate manner in class. The students were only able to express their feelings about the school informally via their parents, teachers, the principal, or the rabbi.

A printed curriculum was made available to all families. This eight page handout covered cognitive and affective objectives for all grades for the following subjects: Siddur,[6] Tzedakah, Israel, Holidays, Hebrew, Torah,[7] and Music-Drama-Crafts. It also included in a few paragraphs a discussion of goals and objectives according to grade level. Another seven-page pamphlet, called the "Family Handbook," was sent to families by the school. This handbook briefly described educational goals of the school, included a calendar and a list of school hours and locations, and described school policies on student absence, discipline, and classroom observation. A brief note describing the network of communication was included, as was a description of "family night" and eligibility requirements for Bar/Bat Mitzvah.

Chapter Six

PROBLEMATIC ASSUMPTIONS AND SELF-DECEPTION

Problematic Assumptions

Underlying the school goals, the curriculum, the instruction, and virtually everything about the school were two faulty assumptions (Schoem 1988a,1984a). These assumptions, to be known here as the Jewish "Way of Life" assumption and the Jewish "Community" assumption, were held by the staff members and by a small minority of parents. All of these people understood, at some level, that their assumptions were misleading; however, within the school context and during school hours, these same people carried out the school program and interacted with people at the school based on the premise of the truthfulness of those assumptions.

The Jewish "Way of Life" Assumption

The Jewish "Way of Life," although never explicitly defined, implied some practice beyond the mere ability to identify and acknowledge membership in one's ethnic group or to acknowledge one's historical roots. It suggested a continuity of the historical into the present so that one acted and thought in an ongoing and encompassing cultural present. It meant the performing of specific rituals and traditions and the conducting of one's life according to a Jewish code.

It stated that one formed feelings, beliefs, values, and thoughts according to a framework of Jewish knowledge and understanding. The staff and some parents of the school assumed, therefore, that what was taught was actual, not historical, that it was relevant to students' lives, and that it was certainly representative of the lives of many Jews in their community and throughout America. Furthermore, and perhaps most problematic, was the fact that in the context of the school setting, the staff and certain parents acted and spoke as if they fully believed that they, in their own lives embodied this Jewish "Way of Life," and they entertained the notion that many of their students did as well.

As has been described in previous chapters, neither the staff nor the parents did, in fact, embody the Jewish "Way of Life." It is not surprising, therefore, that in maintaining such a self-deceptive posture at the school, the inconsistency would be glaring. One teacher, for instance, who told the researcher that in her personal life she did not use "Torah, Bible, or prayer," declared that that was precisely what she wanted to teach at the school: "Torah, Bible, prayer—I wouldn't know how else to teach Hebrew school," she said. Another teacher reported that her goal in the school was to "teach them enough Hebrew and prayer so that they can take part in prayers, holidays, and synagogue activities." However, this same teacher had the following to say about her own observances: "I feel uncomfortable in the synagogue and my husband is not interested—so we go very rarely." A third teacher, who in the classroom stressed the importance of adherence to ritual observance of Jewish holidays, said of her personal life, "My Jewishness is not that important to me. I won't close myself off to it, but I'm just not into it now."

In what was a typical classroom lesson, a seventh grade teacher asked the students to describe in what ways the Sabbath differed from the other days of the week. In response to a student's answer that "on the Sabbath we pray," the teacher said, "But you pray every day." In this case not only was the teacher's response completely detached from reality, but the student who answered was also speaking in theoretical terms. Many of the students in the class had not been to a prayer service on the Sabbath for up to six months or more. When the teacher, who managed a restaurant on Friday evenings, then began to speak about "why don't we work on the Sabbath" students giggled incredulously because of the question's absurdity. Clearly, this lesson that was being discussed in first person terms, was, in the students' minds, about a people that was far removed from their own reality.

The students knew very clearly in their own minds that their own lives and their parents' lives were just like those of the non-Jewish families in their neighborhoods. In addition, the student did not share the Jewish "Way of Life" assumption of the school, and many of them found their parents' inconsistency hypocritical. One student expressed deep-felt confusion with the purpose and relevance for her own life of what she was learning at Shalom School. It was with resentment that she said:

> Like even if our class leaned Hebrew, where are we gonna ever speak it— y'know, you're not around enough—2 1/2 hours—to learn a language anyway... Public school is important because that could do with getting a job or something. But with Hebrew school that's not gonna have anything to do with; well, if you learn—but what's it gonna have to do with when you get older. What do you care if Moses crossed the Sea or something? I don't care.

Even though teachers had a distorted view of behavior once inside the environs of their classrooms, they were still able to accurately depict life in Apple River when confronted with individual cases. If asked about the Weinstocks, the Walls, the Millers, or the Finkelsteins, teachers could estimate relatively accurately about their Jewish life. However, their blurred vision about the group and about the community created the conditions for another faulty assumption, this one regarding the Jewish community.

The Jewish "Community" Assumption

The Jewish "Community" notion held that despite the fact that individual families might not be observant or actively involved Jewishly, there still existed a personal, active, vibrant, and supportive Jewish community. Although some members of the staff despised suburban living and others merely recognized the changed conditions suburbia stood for, there was not a clear understanding that any core elements of community life had changed for the Jewish people there. The staff still assumed that Jewish families gathered for holidays, that the children had Jewish friends, that as a whole the community still had a strong feeling about the Sabbath day, and that people were actively involved in Jewish organizations. This image of community was comprised not of individual persons or families—the staff knew that most individual cases didn't fit the image—but of a general faceless impression that such a community did exist.

In the classroom, the teachers incorrectly assumed that most of their students were knowledgeable about Jewish current events, that they were active or at least belonged to Jewish youth groups, and that they had a Jewish peer group outside of Shalom School. As a result, they were shocked when their students did not know who the Palestinians or the Prime Minister of Israel were, when they were unfamiliar with Jewish communal celebrations, or when they simply wanted to spend some social time with their Jewish friends instead of studying. Issues of community were not even addressed by the curriculum because it was assumed that the community was in good order and that students were participating in other community-oriented organizations.

The Social Environment

Marshall McLuhan's work (1967) originally pointed to the influence and power of the medium itself in transmitting all types of information. Looking at schools, Dreeben (1968) suggested that students in schools learn an assortment of socialization information beyond that which is included in the cognitive curriculum. Studies and essays on schools of different cultures and nations (Hostetler and Huntington 1971; Carnoy 1974; Nyerere 1968; Parsons 1959) have also indicated that the environment of the school may have an important influence in developing individuals who will be able to become full and active participants in that culture or nation.

Competing Influences: Jewish and Secular

At Shalom School, one very important message of the environment was that everyone there was Jewish and their purpose in being there had to do with their being Jewish. (An exception was the secretarial and janitorial workers who were not Jewish.) That, in and of itself, was a significant departure from most of these people's lives.

Another special feature of the school that many people noticed was that the content of the curriculum was made up of Jewish subjects. The student recognized that they learned Hebrew, rather than English as was the case at public school, and they also learned Bible and Jewish history. The students also noticed that some of their books were written in Hebrew and that those books read from right to left, the opposite of English books.

For the most part, however, there was neither recognition of nor a desire for the Jewish school environment to be any different from the public school environment. Ackerman (1978:61) has ruefully noted this circumstance in other Jewish schools as well. He comments:

> The quality of life in the Jewish school is not significantly different from that of the public school. Although we do not have a detailed ethnography of the afternoon school, anyone acquainted with that institution knows that it is, by and large, governed by rules, practices and procedures which are remarkably like those which regulate life in non-Jewish schools. That is a painful paradox: the Jewish religious school attempt to transmit a set of norms and values which are presented as unique and different but patterns its own behavior after a manner rooted in another tradition. If the Jewish religious school is to successfully fulfill its function of socialization for Jewish life, it must itself serve as an exemplar of Jewish living. Life in the school in all its varied aspects must be informed by principles drawn from the Jewish tradition.

It was the principal's opinion, however, that "school should be looked at as a business." To a fourth grade student, what stood out most to her about the Jewish school was that "It's mostly just a school." A fifth grader said, "I don't feel any more Jewish in this school than my public school." Indeed, there was no recognition of an atmosphere, or feeling in the school that was a Jewish atmosphere or Jewish feeling. There was no mention or indication that people interacted with one another—teacher to student, principal to teacher, parent to teacher—in any special manner except that there was an absence of anti-semitic fears. Finally, the physical setting of the school also did not add any sense of Jewishness to the school.

To some extent, the school attempted to schedule its program according to the Jewish calendar. However, compromises were made in accordance with public school calendars. Significantly, the school began in September and ended in early June as did the public schools. The school closed not only for Jewish holidays, but for public school vacations and national holiday weekends. The school resisted closing for such days as Halloween but its attendance marked a sharp decrease on these days.

The rabbi was insistent that students wear head coverings, or Keepoat, during school hours as one action in this direction. Particularly at the beginning of the school year, the rabbi distributed Keepoat to each teacher prior to the start of every class. However, the ambivalence and disinterest on the part of teachers and a disinterest on the part of students made for even this practice to be only spotty in a few classes and nonexistent in most others shortly after the start of the year.

It was also noted, by staff, parents, and students alike, that conditions at the school were "looser" than at public school. Discipline it was felt, was not rigorously enforced, and high academic standards, many noted, were not demanded. Although some students mentioned that they felt safer physically at Shalom School than at their public schools, many students also revealed that their own behavior was considerably less disciplined at Shalom School. The "loose" standards were not intended as policy by the staff or school board and was not a misreading of an open education approach at the school. It seemed, rather, that the relaxation of standards came from an attitude that viewed the Shalom School as being not a terribly serious endeavor and certainly far less important than public school.

The most obvious perceived evidence that Shalom School was not of equal importance to public school was the negative comparison in terms of hours of class time. There was also a widespread acknowledgement that because public school achievement was tied to future career rewards it was of greater importance. In the context of discussions on the relationship of grades and discipline, the comments of two students on two separate occasions illustrated the perceived value of a Jewish education. One student said,

> Kids don't act this way in regular school. Because it's after school and you don't get a grade or anything. But if they gave grades it wouldn't matter because it doesn't count for anything.

Another student's comment was:

> Grades wouldn't do any good. Who cares if you get an "F" in Hebrew School. It won't stop you from getting into college.

Many parents noted with dismay the fact that the school did not have grades, give tests, or stress competition on a par with the public schools. The rabbi argued that this approach was used to teach students responsibility for knowledge by learning to share it. The parents, however, viewed their absence as being more a part of the "looseness" in the school rather than an "approach." The rabbi also believed that the school was unique in its encouragement of open discussion of values and beliefs in the classroom. This aspect of instruction, however, was rarely evident at the classroom level.

In believing that "a school is a school" people had in mind the American public school as their model. It demonstrated the degree to which people had lost any sense of uniqueness or distinction about a Jewish culture. It also suggested the close fit that people felt between themselves and what they perceived as American cultural patterns, and the strong identificational bonds they felt with American socializing institutions.

The Part-Time Metaphor*

In time, money, attitude, and commitment, the Shalom School was a part-time endeavor (Schoem, 1988a). The few hours that the school met represented that time when Jews of Apple River "stepped out" of their daily lives to be and to act Jewish. Being Jewish, except for their survival fears, was indeed a part-time concern. So, too, were most people only concerned about the school in terms of maintenance and survival, while putting it out of their minds most other times. One school board member described the degree of their concern:

> Parents are not very interested in religious school unless there is a crisis. For instance, they did come for the seventh grade meeting [an emergency meeting]. They stopped their tennis games and came. But I don't think there has been much communication beyond that.

When students talked about "school" among themselves, the reference was always to their public school, never the Jewish school. One student who no longer attended Shalom School explained that "when I went, Hebrew school didn't really count—oh, it's just Hebrew school." A seventh grader also spoke of the limited value attached to Shalom School:

> It doesn't really matter to me. If we learned something really interesting, then, maybe, I would want to go more. But the way it is now, I'd rather go bowling.

A third student commented that she was "not even sure all the teachers want to be there."

Because it was an experience that was not integrated into their daily lives, the school was described by both students and parents as being inconvenient in that it interfered with their daily routine. The Sunday morning hours deprived students of their free time and the weekday afternoon school hours prevented them from participating in public school sports and clubs or from doing as their non-Jewish friends did at that time. Describing the problem of weekday classes, one student said:

> It's too long. You get home from school and then right away you have to go to Hebrew school. And then you eat dinner, and sometimes there's no time for homework.

Living in the business world of capitalist America, the synagogue board saw to it that the synagogue's finances were organized according to business principles. It was permissible for the rabbi and principal, etc. to talk about Jewish values, but only after the financial structure was secured according to business values.

---

*Reprinted from *Persistence and Flexibility: Anthropological Perspectives on the American Jewish Experience* by Walter Zenner, editor, by permission of the State University of New York Press. © 1988 State University of New York

Using this business sense, the members of the synagogue board viewed the school as a costly drain of dollars, particularly for a part-time program whose financial return, at best, was only the Bar/Bat Mitzvah. Their monetary investment, therefore, was aimed at school maintenance rather than educational excellence. By refusing to equate, in any sense, educational quality with monetary expenditure, the school went along with underemployed teachers, inadequate facilities, and limited numbers of employees until the very survival of the school came into question. At that point, small adjustments were made to insure its survival, yet the board's primary consideration continued to be one of: "We can fill the market cheap."

Given a part-time staff, the school was led by people who necessarily had other full-time concerns. One teacher, who had two other part-time teaching jobs, a weekend youth group position, and attended college full-time, remarked, "I sleep in my spare time." Another teacher, who was resentful that she "had no time for myself," ranked her teaching position after her half-time sales position, and her full-time studies. Another teacher worked part-time as a construction worker; a fourth as a full-time donut shop clerk; a fifth bought and opened a restaurant during the course of the school year. One teacher explained that she took the teaching position at Shalom School only "because I didn't have another job. I like to teach but I would prefer an all-day school or public school," she said. As a result of their busy schedules and the demands of their more full-time concerns, adequate classroom preparation, even any at all, was an infrequent occurrence for many. Often the day's lesson plan was created in the carpool while driving to work. The principal, too, was bound by another half-time position. After working for four years in a full-time capacity but at half-time pay, she had finally decided to work where she would be paid for her extra time. However, limiting her time at Shalom School more closely to the agreements of her contract left many things undone that she felt were essential. Envisioning herself as a full-time person, she said, "if we could, we would have family weekend retreats, take the kids to Israel, have weekend retreats, field trips—but as a part-time person I can't do it."

Finally, the limited meeting hours of school—two or three times per week for a total of four to five and one-half hours—created additional difficulties. For one thing, there was a rushed sense about the school. The lack of time made it difficult for deep relationships to develop between student and teacher, teacher and teachers, principal and teacher, etc. Directions, instructions, even casual conversations were conducted in a hurried manner. Class projects that initially drew interest from students became boring to them as it took weeks and weeks to accomplish tasks that demanded only a few hours. Teachers found themselves almost immediately falling behind in material that they already realized could be taught in only the most superficial manner. Considerable time was spent every class session reviewing that which the students did not learn in their previous lessons. The limited time also inhibited the possibility of intensity or deep involvement in any class session, as did the hungry and tired feeling students had on weekdays coming after a full day of studying in public school. One fifth grade student remarked:

> At public school we do things all day; I really get into it. Hebrew school is too short to get into it. It's hard to go to Hebrew school after public school.

In a never ending cycle, these part-time temporal and material constraints fed and reinforced the part-time attitudes and assumptions that in turn refueled the temporal and material constraints ad infinitum. The limited emotional investment in the school led to a limited monetary investment which led to a "looseness" in administrative policies and standards. That was reinforced by inadequate and unprepared teachers and students who came without interest and left bored. Implied was the understanding that a full-time commitment could not or would not be made to a part-time program, particularly one that was only a part-time concern.

School Finances — Business Ethics and Priorities

Every family that chose to send their children to Shalom School had to become members of the Shalom Synagogue. In addition to paying their membership the family paid an additional but much smaller sum as tuition for each child enrolled in the school. The synagogue, in turn, used the school tuition payments and a portion of its total income to cover school expenses. Tuition payments accounted for forty-five percent of the school budget with the remainder representing twenty-eight percent of the total income from membership dues.

Within the synagogue the prevailing attitude was that the synagogue had an obligation to help pay for the school. The minority objection to this viewpoint was that members with no children in the school were forced to contribute to the school without, in some sense, any return on their money. Regardless of viewpoint, however, both groups pictured the school as an entity in many ways not integrally connected to the synagogue within the budgetary context.

From another perspective, not considered at the synagogue, the school could have been viewed as a major financial boon for the synagogue. Many members openly admitted that they only joined the synagogue because of the school, and others, who claimed they would have joined anyway, waited to join until their children were of school age. In addition, most of those who joined because of their children's Jewish education remained members even after their children completed or dropped out of school. Himmelfarb (1976) and Waxman (1976) have written and disagreed on the degree of impact that synagogue schools may have on membership enrollments, and certainly it is possible to conjecture that without the lure of the school, other rituals tied to membership such as Bar/Bat Mitzvah or the lack of special tie-ins might attract equal numbers of members. Nevertheless, the indication of many families at Shalom Synagogue was that given the present structure, they

Problematic Assumptions and Self-Deception 71

would have preferred not to have joined the synagogue both out of a concern for monetary savings and, for some, simply out of a lack of interest. As one parent remarked:

> That Sunday school would have a lot more children enrolled if you didn't have to belong to the Temple. A lot of people I know want to send their kids to Hebrew school and want the same things I want, but they don't happen to have [x$Dollars] per year; or [they say] it doesn't offer anything to me—just the Sunday school—why spend [x$Dollars]?

Given the predominant perspective held by most synagogue board members, the school was considered an important and costly arm of the synagogue but, at the same time, was only one of several synagogue priorities. Two issues dominated debates over finances of the school. First, some questioned whether quality education was an objective of the school, and second, whether increased funding would necessarily result in improved quality. In an important budgetary discussion, an influential member of the congregation board raised the first question. He said:

> Does the congregation really want quality education? Maybe we just want kids to make it through their Bar Mitzvah.

Although most board members did not dare be as frank as the person quoted above, since it was normatively understood that Jews were always supposed to be in favor of education, many supported his budgetary position by saying:

> There are a lot of things we'd like to have in life but we have to limit ourselves.

In most of the areas in which school administrators recognized problems that might be solved by money, such as the school buildings, school supplies, and the quality of teachers, the synagogue board grudgingly increased its budget only enough to try to keep pace with inflation. An exception, after a bitter political struggle, was the decision of the board to double the principal's salary in order to make the position full-time.

It was with a business ethic as their guide, assiduously learned at their workplace, that the board considered the financial matters of the school. In contrast to what those at the school wanted to teach as Jewish values, the chief value and priority of the board was the dollar. Other values, such as people, education, or "the golden rule," were not discarded; they were just secondary in importance. In doubling the salary of the principal for the coming year, the salary was still considerably lower than the average income of the heads of households living in Apple River. (The status of the principal, who had worked over forty hours per week while hired at a minimal half-time salary for the past four years, was revealed in her answer "I am embarrassed to tell you" when first asked about her salary by the researcher.) Furthermore, the board argued that the person hired as full-time principal would be expected to fully complete the job, regardless of whether it took forty or sixty hours to do so. There was even criticism of those, including the rabbi, who might have suggested to the current half-time principal that she need not feel pressured to work more than fifty-percent time. The principal herself, however, carried this very same type of attitude to her own staff, stating, "It seems incredible that we have to pay these prices, but it's competition and inflation."

On a different level, one teacher came in tears to a school board meeting at the start of the school year, crying that the synagogue had arbitrarily deducted a large sum of her salary to pay for her overdue membership dues. Another teacher reported that while she personally had no financial complaints with Shalom School, she had been shocked at the other Jewish school where she taught when she found that she was not alone in facing broken verbal agreements, re-interpreted contracts, and subsequent reduced paychecks. It seemed that at the Jewish school the pretense of the Jewish "Way of Life" was not permitted to extend itself outside the classroom in a whole assortment of areas. School finances were indeed one area that the synagogue community very clearly did not want to have influenced by consideration of Jewish values.

Administrative Organization

The rabbi, the principal, and the school board, according to the organizational structure, were considered largely responsible for the administrative and decision-making functions of Shalom School. In practice, it was the rabbi who was most responsible for policy decisions and the principal who was most responsible for carrying them out. Although the school board chairperson was included in many decisions, the school board, it seemed, functioned primarily as a cooling-out body for interested persons with negatively critical input. The synagogue board, which had ultimate authority for all programs of the synagogue, heard regular reports from the school board chairperson and gave final approval to the school budget. It was the parents, in addition to the rabbi and principal, who comprised the school board. They also had avenues of input through direct verbal conversation with the rabbi, the principal, or the teachers, and through service as a room mother/father. Teachers, while having input to policy makers primarily through discussions with the principal, in fact, had considerable freedom within the confines of the classroom. Students had only the informal avenues of input through discussions with parents, teachers, the principal, or the rabbi.

The Rabbi: Ultimate Authority

Although it was the rabbi who commented, "There is a limited hierarchy but we try not to emphasize it—it's not part of the value system we want," most everyone in the school and synagogue understood that the rabbi was at the top of the hierarchy and was the guiding force behind the school. His authority was widely accepted largely because he was well-liked by the parents and students, and because, as one teacher put it, "A rabbi is an educator, I think, by definition, although not all rabbis really are." Another teacher correctly observed that this "rabbi sets the standard and the community must follow along." The principal, who often shared in decision-making with the rabbi periodically referred those who disagreed with her decisions to see the rabbi, as he was the ultimate authority. While the rabbi's greatest interest in the school seemed to be in matters regarding teaching and curriculum, the school board frequently refused to even discuss non-substantive administrative details without him present. Parents who desired greater input, however often felt very frustrated. These parents related experiences with the rabbi in which they felt he had merely tried to pacify them or told them "cool it!" One parent's impression was that the attitude of the rabbi and principal was, "This is the way it's going to be, period!" While the rabbi was frequently present at the school grounds and taught a class to both the seventh graders and to the high school students, the teachers felt that he kept his distance from them. One teacher recalled that the rabbi had not been available the first two years that she had worked at the school, and another said, "He seems really unapproachable for some reason. He seems really caught up in being a rabbi."

The School Board: Cooling Out Function

The school board officially represented the voice of lay people in school affairs and was authorized with the power to make decisions. In practice, however, it was a rubber stamp organization acceding to the wishes of the rabbi and principal. This fact was attested to by members of the board in years past who had eventually become frustrated and resigned, and by the fact that it was the principal who recommended the appointment of the school board chairperson. While school board meetings were run by the chairperson, the principal provided their major source of information about the school and the rabbi provided definitive policy. One new member, who resigned after one session, was a graduate of Shalom School and had hoped to have an impact on policy at the school by serving on the board. What she experienced, however, was something quite different than she expected. She said,

> Something was lacking in the school and I thought that maybe I could get something going, y'know, the education I got there wasn't good enough for me. I wanted to learn more—it wasn't intense enough—it was Mickey Mouse.
>
> The first meeting I went to, well, that just wasn't what the education committee was all about, I thought they were gonna talk about the curriculum, and how they teach, and what's going on, but it wasn't. They talked about money and attendance.

Indeed, among the matters considered by the board were the recording of attendance, providing lunch at the teacher's orientation, and sponsoring a candy sale to raise extra school funds. Even the school board chairperson, upon reflection, questioned the importance of her committee. She said,

I often think to myself, why do I have these meetings; what are they for, anyway? When I plan out my agenda I see, well there's not a whole lot to discuss. And even if we do discuss it, what's going to happen—nothing!

The school board did consider other matters, such as the budget, the rehiring of the principal, and a change in the school location, but these issues were actually resolved in preliminary meetings with the rabbi, principal, and school board chairperson. With respect to the above issues and other critical issues that presented themselves during the school year, it seemed that the rabbi and principal were able to present their own decisions and opinions to the parents yet deflect direct criticism at themselves by using the school board as their mouth piece. In one instance, the principal even told the teachers that the school board had voted to fire them for lateness when the school board had never even taken a vote on the matter.

Perhaps the main purpose served by the school board, however, was to "cool out" views opposed to those of the rabbi and principal regarding the school. Since the school board was the institutional vehicle for parental input, critical parents could be and were directed by the administration to serve on the committee to voice their complaints, fully aware that most parents would not or could not put in the time to do so. At the same time, those serving on the school board were socialized to defend the school's policies since they were now supposedly making those policy decisions themselves. Members of the school board, in fact acted as staunch supporters of the school whether as a group or as individuals at public meetings, parent-teacher conferences, or on a one-to-one basis. Reflecting on a meeting of seventh grade parents that was called by the school board to discuss discipline problems, one parent stated, "At the seventh grade parents meeting, the parents were all saying one thing, and they [the school board, rabbi, and principal] were all saying another thing." At a heated, emotional school board meeting at the end of the year, held open to all parents to "officially" hear their opinions, one parent, angry and frustrated, stated,

We said these same things three years ago and there has been no change. The problem was discipline then and it is now. We had the same questions and answers and there has been nothing done. I don't know why we have these meetings.

At the close of the meeting came these comments from the principal and the school board chairperson, respectively:

We heard you tonight and we will try to make some changes.

Come to the school board meetings.

The Principal: Visible and Accountable

The principal of the school, responsible in her half-time position for bringing together in an organized fashion all of the people and parts making up the school, was the individual most visible and held most accountable by all those associated with the school. Trained as a teacher (she had a masters degree in education) with some experience in inner city schools, the principal had become involved in Jewish education because "I felt I should work with Jewish kids in education." She felt a personal pride in the fact that the Shalom School had grown from 135 to 250 students during her term as principal; nevertheless, she admitted that her major strength as an educator was not in the area of administration. Perhaps as a result of this concern, as well as her time constraints, the principal devoted almost all of her time to matters of bureaucratic detail at the expense of areas that she preferred, such as curriculum development and teacher supervision. One teacher who noted this, stated,

> She's pretty unorganized. She gets too wrapped up in administration although I think she would like to work more with teachers.

The principal began the school year with some serious apprehension. One of her major concerns was that on top of caring for her two young children, she was teaching half-day everyday at a Jewish all-day school. In previous years she had allowed herself to work full-time for a half-time salary at Shalom School, but this year decided her family needed additional income. A second concern of the principal was her job security at Shalom School. Early in the year she decided that she would only continue working there in future years as a full-time professional and had deep-rooted fears that if a full-time appointment were made, she would be denied the position. Her third concern was that of being intimidated and being unable to work with the newly appointed administrative assistant, a former principal of the school, wife of the synagogue's powerful treasurer, and a strong-willed individual herself. During the course of the year all of these apprehensions were, in fact, realized. The principal was not only exhausted and harassed when arriving at Shalom School after a full morning of teaching but she found the Shalom School position impossible to complete in twenty hours per week; she was the focus of a strong, sometimes bitter effort not to rehire her; and she was in a constant state of anxiety in the presence of her administrative assistant.

While the principal was well-liked as a person, there was a widespread opinion that both she and the school were badly disorganized. Some did not find the disorganization too problematic, but others were incensed at the air of disorder at the school. Typical of the varying feelings of distress about the disorganization were these comments:

> I like her [the principal], but I've seen more together principals and people.

> [The principal] is terrific but the school has a harassed atmosphere.

> If she didn't have her head attached she'd forget that, too.

> There is an aura of disorganization that is rampant.

The effect of administrative difficulties were felt in a number of areas. One persistent problem that plagued the school was a lack of respect for school policy in the form of chronic teacher lateness and widespread disregard for behavioral standards on the part of students. Due to teacher lateness, classes regularly began ten to fifteen minutes late, representing a loss of five to fifteen percent of school time each session. On one of these "late" starting days, one student commented to the researcher:

> Isn't this a funny school? The kids are all here but the teachers don't come to class.

An enforced administrative policy, which stated that no student could be suspended or expelled from school, seemed to undermine both the teachers' and the principal's power to discipline students. Art supplies, books, chalk, etc. were frequently in short supply or hard to find when the teachers needed those items. Assembly programs and group activities were not infrequently upset by performers canceling or speakers arriving late and the school was never ready with adequate backup plans. Classroom interruptions, sometimes numbering over ten per session, plagued the teachers throughout the year. These interruptions were defined as a person walking into the class after the start of school, and the people most responsible were other teachers, the rabbi, the principal, and the school board chairperson.

Teachers: Selection and Supervision

Although the principal spoke of being selective in her choice of teachers, the experience of candidates for teaching positions indicated that this aspect of the school was equally disorganized. While the principal did admit that she felt her choice of teachers was too limited, three teachers who were hired related the impression that the school was actually desperate for teachers. They reported that the interviews of two of them were for less than ten minutes, and that their second interview with the rabbi was even shorter, or took place in the street, or did not take place at all. In commenting on the criteria used to hire them, these teachers responded as follows:

> They were desperate.

> I felt I had the job before the interview.

> A teacher had finked out and she [the principal] was in a spot.

A major area of concern for teachers once they were hired was a feeling of being abandoned by the principal in terms of support and guidance. In her absence, a number of teachers repeatedly approached the researcher looking for new teaching strategies, and feedback on their classroom instruction. One new teacher expressed concern that while he had had experience leading youth groups he was not an experienced teacher and needed direction. Another teacher who was fired/resigned during the first weeks of school had told the researcher during her tenure there of her increasing anxiety as a teacher in the classroom without any perceived support system. One teacher who was experienced and felt more comfortable in the classroom explained that the principal "has a habit of giving advice after the thing is done." Some teachers however liked the freedom they gained as a result of the principal's lack of supervision because, as one said, "I can do whatever I want to do."

Another administrative problem that existed between the principal and her teachers was in the area of communication of information. From the first day of school, when the students had to show the teachers where to enter the building and the teachers saw their classroom for the first time, there was little time provided for planning or preparation. Teachers were told to choose their elective course topic during the middle of class time while the principal stood waiting in the doorway; library time was scheduled when the librarian came knocking unannounced; a mimeographed sheet giving instructions for a holiday activity to begin on a Sunday morning was distributed to teachers at the start of class on Sunday morning; and finally, teachers never seemed aware when teacher's meetings were to occur.

Facilities Problems

As described in chapter five, the total schedule of classes at Shalom School took place on three days and at three separate locations. The school planned to have its own building on the synagogue property in the future, but, in the meantime it attempted to make do with what was available. The most difficult problem that existed because of the lack of a single building was coordination of grades K-3 in one location with the program for grades 4-7 at another on Sunday mornings. The principal, whose only office space (even it was shared with other synagogue personnel) was located at the third building, attempted to be at both locations on Sunday. Her driving time, clocked by the researcher one Sunday morning, was thirty-five minutes for the round trip. This driving time represented almost one-fourth of the entire 150 minute session on Sunday morning. In addition there were either structural, acoustical, and/or furniture problems in each of four different classrooms. One class was held in a very large social hall and sounds echoed off the walls. The classroom below that class heard footsteps from above in magnified form. The third room was furnished as a lounge rather than a classroom, and a fourth room was not adequately insulated for very cold days.

The rabbi, principal, and school board members perceived these physical problems to be the root cause of difficulties in the school. The rabbi expressed this feeling, saying:

> It's impossible—impossible because we don't have one building and parents can't stand going to two buildings; and we spend all of our time coordinating and running from place to place that we can't deal with the substantive issues.

Indeed, this group felt confused and overwhelmed by these physical difficulties, particularly because the greatest amount of time any one person devoted to the school was the half-time principal. Some parents and teachers, on the other hand, believed that the multiple locations posed such a problem only because of administrative ineptitude. Nevertheless, it did provide these administrators with an external excuse for many types of school problems, even if it was of questionable validity in certain cases.

In the minds of the parents and students, however, the physical problems were an annoyance but were not a barrier to quality education. The parents felt, in fact, that it was they who carried the burden of the problem by having to transport their younger children and older children to different locations on Sunday mornings. However, they believed that once the students were in class, there was no reason that the different locations should pose any further disruption. One parent verbalized this feeling, saying:

> The building is the least important thing. I'm against fighting over the school building and not talking about curriculum.

Discipline problems in the class meeting in the large social hall prevented the minimizing of the acoustic problem there. In the class below the social hall the sound of crashing footsteps periodically interrupted and annoyed both teacher and students but did not interfere with the class as a whole. Finally, the teacher with the lounge furniture attempted to work with the room's design to make his class more informal, and the improperly insulated classroom posed only infrequent problems. Nevertheless, each of these interruptions and annoyances, added to other difficulties in the school, only made things more difficult and made people less patient and less agreeable.

One of the major changes proposed for the next school year by the school board was to make greater use of the converted school building at the synagogue in place of the Jewish Community Center Building. This move was intended to cut down driving time between buildings on Sunday, and facilitate a closer connection between school and synagogue. However, it also meant the break-up of several classes in grades 4-7 because in order to accommodate students at the synagogue building the school was to be open more days but with fewer students attending on any given day.

The administrative problems of the school were part of and added to the negative cycle within the school. In deciding to hire a part-time administrator at the lowest price they could negotiate, the school risked hiring a person whose qualifications in certain aspects of administration were limited. In addition, it was very questionable whether any part-time person could have adequately handled such a job. Furthermore, the external problems of the school such as the physical setting, only made the job that much more difficult for anyone to administer in twenty hours per week. As a result, the aura of disorganization that appeared further fed the "loose" attitude towards the school, which in turn, created the conditions for deciding to only hire a part-time, low paid administrator. Finally, the organizational problems became so overwhelming that the more deeply rooted problems facing the Jewish school were only casually addressed and were often ignored.

Those directing the school fashioned it in terms of their Jewish "Way of Life" assumptions once inside the school walls. However, the overwhelming influence of the American business ethic and the American social structure permeated their own and their synagogue directors' thinking when looking at the school from without. Thus, not only was the administrative organization of the school crippled by material considerations, but the social structure of the school, too, was indelibly etched in American norms and standards. The attempt at that late point, given the nature of the social and organizational structures, to begin to think or teach about a Jewish "Way of Life" within the Shalom School was an effort that to all intents and purposes was already a doomed proposition.

Chapter Seven

A Confusion of Purpose in the Classroom

Developing and Interpreting the Curriculum

The Shalom School and Synagogue were members of the ideological Conservative Movement within Jewish institutional life. While it is true that there were many parents who had chosen to be associated with Shalom School and Synagogue specifically for that very reason, there existed considerable confusion as to what Conservative Judaism stood for. Even one of its leading spokesmen in the country commented on this problem:

> But first the Conservative movement has to put its own house in order... As I see it, this would include among others: articulating a definition of Conservative Judaism which is intelligible and unambiguous... A clear and persuasive definition of Conservative Judaism is needed, not alone to distinguish it from Orthodoxy and Reform, both of which have moved in the direction of the Conservative Movement during the last quarter of a century, but to project the ideal to which Conservatism aspires... What is troubling is that Conservatives have been weakened in the process because of failure to project an unequivocal public definition of Conservative Judaism that is distinguished from watered down Orthodoxy or eclectic Reform. The result is that those who seek authenticity often go elsewhere.
>
> (Lieber 1978)

Religious Ideology and the Influence of the Conservative Movement

The influence of the Conservative movement on education at Shalom School came from its national education branch, responsible for setting standards, publishing textbooks, and developing curricular materials. However, the use of or adherence to any of their work was optional for individual schools and the firm attitude at Shalom School was that "The Conservative Movement has little influence; this is [Shalom School's] Hebrew school." Of a highly publicized new curriculum developed by the Conservative Movement for the Jewish afternoon school, the rabbi said, "A lot of it is junk. It's stuff we found out ten years ago."

Even as the ideology of the Conservative Movement was unclear to its leadership, its members were even more bewildered. "As has been frequently observed," commented the president of the Conservative Movement's (Lieber 1978) University of Judaism, "there are almost no Conservative Jews, only

Conservative rabbis." Most people distinguished Conservative Judaism as being somewhere in-between the more rigid Orthodox and less rigid Reform Movements. In limited observations at afternoon schools of all three movements in the metropolitan area, the major distinction in instruction was the attitude regarding observance of Jewish law. At the Orthodox school students were told that they were commanded by God to obey and observe Jewish laws; at the conservative school students were told that they should observe Jewish laws; finally, at the reform school, students were told they had the individual choice observing if and what they desired. However, from informal discussions with students and teachers, it was clear that the large majority of families of all these schools were observing Jewish laws in a most minimal fashion, if at all.

Another factor that blurred the distinction of these ideologies was that many teachers, who either claimed no commitment to any movement or a weak commitment to one, taught at more than one of the different ideological schools. The attitude of the school board chairperson at Shalom School was that "As long as they are knowledgeable of what they should teach, that's all we can expect of them. We can't ask what they do or believe at home." The principal was similarly uninterested in their association with the religious ideological movements. What she looked for in her teachers was the following: "I think it's important to have young, vibrant minds, a practicing knowledge of Jewish law and tradition, and an awareness of Jewish resources; some practice and identification but not necessarily orthodox or conservative." The teachers themselves were hardly bothered by teaching in the different schools. Their prevailing attitude about the school ideology seemed to be that it was "according to the idiosyncrasies of the rabbi." Furthermore, these teachers felt little if any pressure or reason to conform to different ideological beliefs when moving from conservative to orthodox to reform Jewish afternoon schools.

Partners in the Curriculum

Curriculum is a set of ideas and plans that has many facets beyond the printed word and is perceived differently by people in different roles. The rabbi and principal of Shalom School were very proud of the printed curriculum (see below) that they had developed but thought of it, primarily, in its ideal, printed from. The teachers, however, who were responsible for operationalizing the curriculum in their individual classrooms, had a variety of different interpretations and viewpoints regarding it which were often reflected in their instruction. The students, who were the intended recipients of the substance of the curriculum, further affected the curriculum by bringing to the classroom their own life experience and perspectives. They also evaluated the curriculum in a different way from their own unique position. The parents, too, viewed the curriculum from their own perspective as outside but interested observers, since they were still responsible for funding the school and sending their children to it. In this broader sense, as it was played out by all parties in all its facets in the day-to-day classroom experience, the curriculum

A Confusion of Purpose in the Classroom

was not just a printed document but was a multi-dimensional configuration. It was in this form that it illustrated and brought clarity to the dilemmas, pressures, and difficulties that being an ethnic minority in a pluralistic society entail.

The rabbi and principal believed their curriculum to be the best Jewish afternoon school curriculum in the entire metropolitan area (Schoem 1984a). The principal said of it:

> The curriculum is solid. I am extraordinarily proud of it... We teach the sources. I refuse to go along with all the modish courses that come along every year. I'm not sure we're reaching as many kids as we might, but we're giving them the best quality. We are teaching values. The whole curriculum is value-oriented.

The [Shalom School] Curriculum

This is a guide and a brief introduction to curriculum and philosophy behind your child's education at [Shalom School]. In it we have tried to alert you to the kinds of things your children are studying so that you can reinforce these lessons in your home. We feel that our school is only a small beginning in introducing your children to Jewish identity and values and that without your support we cannot even approach success in achieving our goal—to build a responsive, responsible Jewish community for the future.

We encourage you to examine the curriculum carefully and discuss it with your children. Ask them after each session what they have learned and discuss all of the questions, doubts and misgivings they might have. Only through teamwork amoung (sic) the home, the synagogue and the school can we hope to educate a responsible Jewish community.

> I look froward to meeting all of you and will be glad to discuss any questions or problems you might have.
>
> Shalom U'lihitraot
>
> (Shalom, see you soon)

FOURTH GRADE

In the fourth grade the children begin to attend our school on a two-day-a-week basis: Sundays and Wednesdays. The curriculum takes on a different appearance with emphasis shifting toward Torah, Siddur and social studies. By this time a nucleus of Jewish identity has been formed and the student is ready to discover the tools that help bring self-fulfillment as a Jew. However, the methods and materials used in the process must be varied and exciting. The children are well passed (sic) the age where things are interesting simply because they are new, and creativity must be a key work in this curriculum. Drama, crafts and music must not be neglected are (sic) are still an integral part of the curriculum. The children have singing and dancing with their regular teacher. Drama and crafts are generally introduced where appropriate at the discretion of the teacher.

For Siddur, the fourth grade studies the Friday evening service. They examine the concept of the prayers as well as learning their key Hebrew words. Their Torah lessons are taken from *Chumash Meforash*, and the children are expected to be able to solve textual problems as specified. They acquire some identity with key Biblical figures through role playing and dramatics.

The fourth grade social studies program is centered around the book, *When A Jew Celebrates*.

FIFTH GRADE

The fifth grade continues with *Chumash Meforash* in the area of Torah. The point at which it continues varies from year to year depending on fourth grade progress. It also begins using *Torah Study Units*, a self-directed Torah study program designed and written by Rabbi. This program teaches the students the inquiry process that is so necessary in studying Torah.

The Siddur study in the fifth grade centers around the Kriyat Shema, and the same concept, key-word technique is used.

The social studies program in the fifth grade is centered around Israel as a modern Jewish nation, and how it affects us as Jews. The children will work at the variety of styles of living that Israel provides. Every effort will be made to find them Israeli pen pals. They will plan an imaginary trip to Israel using travel brochures, audio-visual supplements, etc. In this manner, they become familiar with the country's geograph (sic) as well as the history of each city.

SIXTH GRADE

Jews in crisis is the social studies curriculum for the sixth grade. They will examine the plights of Soviet Jewry and Middle Eastern Jewry at present. They will then look back through history at the Jewish predicament in 1492 (The Spanish Inquisition) and the Jew at the time of Shabtai Zvi. They will also consider the situation that Jewish People faced at the time of the Maccabees and also Massada.

The Siddur program centers around the Amidah. The students are also using a new text called *When A Jew Prays*, that raises philosophical and ethical questions about prayer.

The Torah program continues to use *The Torah Study Units*, and continues from where the fifth grade has ended.

SEVENTH GRADE

The seventh grade social studies curriculum is three fold. Students will examine the American Jewish Community at present, and then try to discover why and from where people came to the U.S. As a result, the more specific emphasis will be on the Shtett (sic) or the Eestern (sic) European Jewish community. The holocaust and the reasons that some people chose to come to the U.S. and others to make Aliyah to Israel. (sic)

The seventh grade Siddur curriculum centers around the Torah Service in preparation for B'Nai Mitzvah. The Rabbi also gives a special B'Nai Mitzvah class dealing with the responsibilities of becoming an active member in the Jewish world.

In Torah, the class finishes the Torah unit course of study.

OBJECTIVES
Music, Drama and Crafts K-3
Hebrew
Torah (Chumach)
Siddur (Prayer)
Israel
Tzedakah K-3
Holidays

In attempting to outline the objectives of [Shalom School] it is easiest to enumerate the major areas of our curriculum and state what we are trying to accomplish regardless of the age level. We may have short and long range goals for each grade, but the objectives involved are generally very similar.

HEBREW
<u>Cognitive</u>
1. Ability to read Hebrew
2. Ability to translate key words—especially those repeated frequently in prayer.

<u>Affective</u>
1. Feeling of identity with Jewish people throughout the world through the ability to worship and study in a common language.
2. Appreciation for the special importance of the Hebrew language in Jewish lift (sic) and thought.
3. Increased appreciation of the synagogue service.
4. Increased appreciation of the Chaumash.
5. Regular participation in worship.

TORAH
Cognitive
1. Familiarity with the general structure and framework of the Torah.
2. Familiarity with at least the major personalities and the gaining of understanding and awareness of the problems they faced.
3. An understanding of the Torah's relevance to the present and its usefulness in making ethical decisions.

Affective
1. To understand the moral laws in order to practice them.
2. To increase desire and curiosity aimed at becoming more familiar with the Torah as literature and inspiration.

SIDDUR
Cognitive
1. Understanding of the concepts found in prayers.
2. Rote mastery of signigicant (sic) blessings and prayers.
3. Understanding of the need for prayer.

Affective
1. To have positive attitudes toward prayer and worship.
2. To form habits of personal prayer and attendance at services.

ISRAEL
Cognitive
1. Understand the way of life in Israel and its similarities and differences to ours.
2. See the relationships among Jews throughout the world, especially between Jews in the U.S. and those in Israel.

Affective
1. Develop a sense of identification and responsibility with Jewish life in Israel.
2. Appreciate the ways in which we can help Israel and Israel can help us.
3. Encourage communication with Israelis through pen-pal programs, trips and projects.

From Curriculum to Instruction

Both the principal and rabbi realized, at times, that what they wrote into the curriculum did not necessarily make its way successfully into the students' hearts and minds. Indeed, despite their enthusiasm with what they had developed, they sometimes spoke of the difficulty in achieving all of their goals. The failures that they did recognize, however, were always attributed to people, circumstances, and events external to the school. The rabbi stated:

> I think the afternoon religious school is a failure; and the question is how much or little of a failure we're going to make it. The distractions of the

environment are so great... We don't have enough time with so many different things; and children resent coming, parents driving kids and not sure they want to send kids. The message they get from parents, peers, even teachers, sometimes, about the school is not a positive one. Therefore, failure is built into the system.

Nevertheless, in recognizing problems facing the school, there was no attempt to alter the curriculum to meet changing needs other than in superficial ways. Certainly it seemed that the prevailing attitude of the rabbi and principal was that their curriculum was excellent, but unfortunately, they were lacking the proper circumstances, community, and type of students to whom to teach it. Furthermore, those more serious failings were not considered to be the problem of the school but of external institutions or groups. The rabbi considered the school's domain of problems to be on a different scale, saying:

> Our biggest problem facing us in the future is working mothers and lack of transportation for the kids.

The curriculum underwent major changes in its movement from the printed page to the teacher's instruction. Not only was there disagreement and re-interpretation of what was written, but there was considerable unauthorized individual curriculum development and goal-setting within classrooms. One teacher stated,

> The written down curriculum has no relation to what is being taught and the kids know nothing of what they were supposed to be taught in the years past.

Another teacher agreed, commenting:

> The school is not organized. Every class has a program, but I'm not sure teachers follow the program.

In fact, there was such little supervision, and such a high degree of personal control that a third teacher remarked:

> If I taught Zen Buddhism in the classroom, frankly, I don't think anyone would notice.

One area of the curriculum to which several teachers objected was the teaching of prayer (SIDDUR). One teacher, who progressively decreased the class time spent on this subject, said:

> Teaching prayers to kids who don't go [to religious services] has no effect. Prayers are the symbol of Judaism today, but it's the wrong symbol. And if the kids learn prayers, they think they know Judaism and they really haven't even begun to find it. If it were up to me, I would remove prayer from the curriculum.

The Israeli teacher in the class next door felt even more strongly about prayer and even religion in the curriculum. She said:

> One of the reasons they hate Hebrew school is because of the Siddur. I don't teach strong religion. I cannot teach what I don't believe.

Nevertheless, when this teacher did teach about religion, her approach was not of questioning or understanding the students' lifestyle, but of dictating how one should live according to Jewish law and implying that she herself was a fervent observer of Jewish law.

Another area of disagreement with the curriculum was in the instruction of Hebrew. Most teachers objected to teaching Biblical Hebrew rather than conversational Hebrew but, in this respect, they complied with the printed curriculum although without enthusiasm. Students and parents frequently objected to either the overemphasis or lack of emphasis on Hebrew instruction altogether. Some of their conflicting opinions resulted from the different emphasis of different teachers, some of whom in turn expressed confusion to the researcher over the degree of emphasis that was expected by the administration. There was confusion, too, among teachers whether to include in the teaching of Hebrew, discussion of Jewish values and holidays, etc. Two teachers who discussed this question with the principal came away with very different understandings of their responsibility. However, because of their independence in the classroom, both planned to include the consideration of values in teaching Hebrew; one because of what she thought the principal had said, and the other in spite of what she thought the principal had said.

Finally, there was some disagreement between the administration, teachers, and some parents over the extent of class time to be spent on Israel. Although the study of Israel was included in the fifth grade curriculum, the rabbi and some parents expressed more concern with teaching students to become comfortable as Jews in their American community. They were excited to have Israeli teachers at the school, but they did not necessarily want them to teach about Israel. During the year, the teachers in grades four through seven, however, included three Israelis and also a number of Americans who were giving serious consideration to moving to Israel as a permanent home. These teachers, and some parents who felt as they did, resented deeply the lack of greater emphasis on Israel, and by mid-year made use of the "looseness" in supervision and took it upon themselves to include discussions of Israel in their classes. One of the Israeli teachers said:

> The synagogue has to realize that for the generations to come the place for Jews is Israel. It's very clear cut in my mind. And that is what should be developed in the Hebrew School.

As a result of the teachers' classroom independence, and the written curriculum being followed neither from year-to-year or from session-to-session, parents had only vague notions about what their children were learning and the children themselves were confused as well. One parent who was distressed over this situation, stated:

A Confusion of Purpose in the Classroom   89

I keep asking people if there is a curriculum. I should ask [the principal] but I am reluctant to confront her. I've spoken to [the school board chairperson] a few times. She said it was the problem of a few students....

Teaching and Learning the Cognitive Curriculum

One of the most serious problems facing effective instruction in the classroom was the detachment of things Jewish in the students' daily lives. With the added burden of the Jewish "Way of Life" assumption on the part of teachers, it almost always came as a shock to them to find their students so ignorant of Jewish events, news, issues, and information.

"Stepping Out" To Study

Students in the fifth grade did not know the name of the Prime Minister of Israel; they asked if the June, 1967 war was a civil war (they were just being born at that time), and they knew very little of the Yom Kippur war of 1973. One student, brave enough to guess, stated that the initials P.L.O. (Palestine Liberation Organization) stood for the Peace Liberation Organization. Most students had never heard of the people called the "Palestinians," and a few who did, continued to call them "Palesterians" after two weeks of discussion.

In another similar incident, the fourth grade students were recalling Bible stories at the start of the school year. Although they could only remember bits and pieces of stories, the few students who were participating seemed quite excited. At one point, during a review of the story of Jacob and Esau, the two boys who were providing all the detail for these stories disagreed with one another. The first boy turned to the other, and citing his source of information said, "I saw the movie." The second boy, equally sure of his facts replied, "Well, I saw the movie, too."

Of course, it was not just the students who were "stepping out" of their daily lives to come to Shalom School. In the teachers' carpool to school one afternoon there was a look of great surprise on some of the teachers' face when one mentioned that that day was the Jewish holiday of Tu Bishvat.[8] It was not surprising to find that in the class being observed that day only one of nine students was aware of the holiday.

Curricular Content

Another factor that made learning difficult, according to some parents and teachers, was that the content itself was superficial and too repetitive from year to year. One senior teacher said,

> We're getting more concerned with rattling off prayers than with understanding the meaning. Hebrew is too surface. The other [the values of Jewish identity] is harder.

Another parent spoke of the need for greater honesty in discussing Judaism and Jewish history. He said:

> There is a one-sided view of Judaism taught; not a full, honest approach and this turns kids and adults off. And reading fairytales after awhile is dull. They want to paint the ideal, not the real; not the truth.

A third parent was bitter that her children seemed to know so little about Jewish life and were so miserable at the school. She commented:

> I expected that they would get a Jewish education—Hebrew, holidays, current events, Israel. But they're not getting it. They learn Hanukah every year. They learn the same thing year after year after year... If they study holidays every year, let them go into it more—discuss them—not just the same stories.

Even some of the teachers who were responsible in their own classes for the repetitiveness and superficial instruction, were aware of the debilitating effect that it had on student interest and student learning. A teacher in the younger grades of the school said:

> I don't think you have to say it has to be this way all the time. I don't think you have to learn the blessing twelve years of your life.

Another teacher went as far as to say that she believed students were being disruptive in their behavior precisely because of the vacuous content of the curriculum. She stated:

> I think the kids are justified in misbehaving. Their feeling is that they are getting the same stuff again and again. And it is useless. There really is no continuity to the program.

Teaching Methods

In addition to the content, students and sometimes teachers themselves found fault in the teachers' instructional methods. Common to several teachers was a habit of teaching by rambling lectures and by reading long selections from books. One teacher, who desired group discussion in his class, didn't realize that he consistently cut off discussion by his method of "answering" student opinions and thoughts. He also didn't understand that students in the back of the room could not read his small blackboard writing nor did he recognize that ten year old students might lose interest while learning about one prayer for an entire session. He did realize and feel badly that he didn't have the instructional expertise to pull off a debate on the Middle East that had initially generated great enthusiasm and independent, outside research by students in the class.

Another inexperienced teacher plodded through centuries of Jewish history with names, facts, and figures. Although she realized that her lectures were dull—

it often seemed that even she was bored—she bemoaned the fact that she didn't know any other way to teach the subject. She remarked:

> The way they are supposed to be taught is boring, terribly boring. Here is the curriculum. Teach them the prayers; don't teach them what they mean. Read the Bible with them. Teach them history—the facts, this, that, and the other thing. No one ever told me how to teach history.

A third teacher tried to use individualized study to teach the *Torah Study Units* developed by the rabbi. In doing so, however, he gave no instructions or explanations to the students except to tell them to read a short passage. The students, in turn, were lost without directions, and so they read out loud, talked to one another, rolled on the floor, and fooled around. Instead of spending the day on the Torah Units, the teacher ended up acting as disciplinarian the entire session.

In another example, two other teachers, one with considerable experience, brought their classes together to perform a play for the school on the Passover holiday. There was never any discussion of the play or its meaning, or of Passover. The students were merely given scripts (there was an insufficient number), told to choose parts, and only later were told that they would perform before others. On the day of the performance only a handful of students wore costumes, several students laughed through their parts, and neither teacher was present because they had made travel plans to be with family for the holiday.

Boredom

One of the most commonly expressed emotions used to describe the students' experience at Jewish school was boredom. Although it was primarily students who talked about being bored, a few teachers and parents accepted their talk as accurately depicting their feelings. One teacher stated:

> The kids—they are bored. I think there must be something behind it. I don't see them going on field trips. I don't see them doing different things that they could be doing. HAVE A FUN ACTIVITY! You know, you can go to a bagel factory and learn more in those two hours; have the kids ever been to a kosher butcher shop?

One parent with two children in the school concurred, sadly commenting, "I think the school is just plain boring for the kids." The students themselves were very certain that they were feeling bored at Shalom School. Typical of the student attitude was the comment that "people don't usually listen because it's boring." One student who blamed the boredom on the repetition of instruction, explained how he and his friends experienced Shalom School:

> Pre-K is the only important class. After that they just teach you the same thing over again and over again and over again and over again. That's why everyone is bored. Like today, nobody answered the question because we all knew it and it's the same thing. We're just bored of it.

Other students felt that part of the problem lay with the teachers' inability to present their material in an interesting manner. One girl said:

> Everyone talks and laughs and talk among themselves and don't listen; because the teacher is boring. He doesn't do anything that we would want to listen to.

Some students suggested that they would prefer "not just listening but doing things and working with others." One sixth grader said that he had "nothing against the teachers, but if you did things in a fun way it would be a lot easier to learn it."

Most parents, however, either discounted their children's complaints out of hand, or simply rejected their children's right to complain. Those who discounted their children's opinions attributed their remarks to either peer pressure or just "kids talking." Other parents felt it was their children's responsibility to enjoy school or not, and not a necessary concern of the school. One parent who told his daughter, "I don't care if you like the teacher," commented that it was "the kid's problem, not the teacher's problem." Another parent simply rejected out of hand the question of enjoying school. Her attitude was that "Hebrew school is not really for liking; you just have to go." The attitude of the school board chairperson was typical of many other parents. She said:

> It's not our responsibility to entertain them. It's not an entertaining situation. It's a school.

Assessing Content Learning

Given an understanding of what was stated as the cognitive curriculum, and how that material was presented, an important remaining question was what and how much of the cognitive curriculum was learned. Ackerman (1969:22) has reported that nationwide the results were discouraging if not disastrous.

> A recent study shows that even when pupils complete the requirements established by the curriculum, they have no recognizable fluency in Hebrew and cannot understand more than carefully edited texts based on a limited vocabulary. Caught in the crossfire of bible study as an independent subject and the use of the biblical text, and an abridged one at that, as a Hebrew language workbook, the pupils learn neither. Despite the fact that close to 50 percent of the instructional time is devoted to the study of Hebrew and Chumash [Torah], the pupil leaves the school upon graduation with only the most infantile notions of biblical thought and ideas, and a capability in Hebrew which hardly goes beyond the monosyllabic responses to carefully worded questions. The study of history is a pious wish, restricted as it usually is to less than one hour a week. Understanding and generalization fall prey to the hurried accumulation of disconnected fact...the hopeless proliferation of subject matter denies even the most competent and dedicated teacher the possibility of significant achievement in any one area.

The indication of this study confirms Ackerman's report that startlingly little cognitive material was being learned. Although this research did not utilize any standardized (there were none used at the school) or independently written achievement tests, it was difficult not to recognize the immensity of the problem. Students in the sixth grade did not know words being taught in the second grade and the most basic terms of holidays, historical events and religious observance were forgotten year after year and from week to week. Teachers were constantly dumbfounded in class by student ignorance of a core of the most elementary cultural information and students neither studied nor did homework. Only a small percentage of students paid attention during class and only a very few participated. Finally, the teachers and students recognized and admitted that students were not learning the cognitive material to any acceptable degree or standard.

The comments of the students and teachers were instructive. The students expressed disappointment, anger, and rebelliousness at not learning; the teachers spoke out of a deep sense of frustration, hopelessness, and despair. One of the bright rebellious students revealed her confusion and ambivalence about the school in evaluating her experience there. She said:

> We don't learn to read. We haven't learned since third grade. We don't know what anything means. It's nice to be able to follow the service, but I don't know what it means. I think Hebrew school is dumb. I mean, we don't learn anything. Like right now, me and my friends are sitting back there writing notes to one another and talking, and the teacher is just having a conversation with herself. You see, I like it this way, but if this is all we're doing, I don't see the point in coming.

Some of the students tried hard to get something more out of their experience, but, like the following student indicated, they were not satisfied.

> I don't really learn anything. Sometimes we look up answers but we don't remember anything. I told the teacher we shouldn't do it that way. I like discussions, though, but we don't have too many of those.

Other students merely accepted the fact that they were not going to learn very much at Shalom School. In considering continuing their Jewish studies after their Bar and Bat Mitzvahs, they told the researcher:

> But if it continued like this I don't think it would be necessary to go anymore because we don't learn very much.

> My mom says I can quit after Bar Mitzvah because I don't think I will learn anymore.

Despite their realization that their transmission of cognitive material was largely unsuccessful, the teachers did not feel that they could pass on this information to the parents. One teacher approached the researcher with his dilemma of what to write on his students' evaluations when he felt that they had learned practically nothing in the past evaluation period. He sighed:

> You can't write an evaluation saying, 'Your child makes trouble and has not learned one thing this year.' You have to put this in nice terms.

Another experienced teacher, blamed the curriculum as the cause of her students' complaining that "I cannot understand; I do not want to come; I don't know how to read; I don't want to write; I don't know what is going on in class," but continued to be surprised that students could not meet even her most minimal expectations. She said:

> By four grades you expect them to know something. But really, they don't know anything—I don't mean anything, but very little. You expect children to read in fourth grade. But they don't know!

Perhaps most indicative of the classroom experience and curricular failure was the emotional comment of one devoted teacher. Exasperated, she exclaimed:

> Everyday I came back from the school I had a heart attack because I hadn't accomplished anything.

Another teacher thought that the entire school program, content and structure combined, was worthless and was in need of a complete overhauling. Of the present school he said:

> I would abolish it. Instead of giving them a fraudulent Jewish education you should give them a proper, more intensive Jewish education.

The examination of the program of curriculum instruction in the cognitive domain at the Shalom School only tends to reinforce both Ackerman's report (1969) and the results of the study by Dushkin and Engelman (1959) nearly three decades earlier. The unavoidable conclusion is that Jewish afternoon schools are not and have not for at least twenty years been able to adequately transmit Jewish content. The sense of failure in this area, expressed twenty years earlier by Dushkin and Engelman (1959:28) still seems relevant, at least as far as the Shalom School was concerned.

> The oft expressed attitude of 'what's the use; after all these years the children know nothing,' may be an exaggeration, but for many American Jews it is a discouraging reality.

Teaching and Learning the Affective Curriculum

Although affective objectives were written for the curriculum in the same manner as cognitive objectives the experience of the classroom once again provided a different picture of that curriculum. While indeed there was success in developing Jewish identification (see Chapter Nine), in the rest of the affective curriculum what was presented was a feeling of ambivalence and ambiguity and what was gained, at best, was a high degree of confusion.

"Stepping Out" As Role Models

In keeping with the Jewish "Way of Life" assumption, the teachers attempted to present to their students an image that indicated a normative standard in approach to things Jewish within Conservative Judaism. The teachers also implied to their students that as individuals each teacher lived according to those normative standards. While allowing for some minor exceptions, they also implied that as a group there was a high degree of uniformity both in opinion and behavior in these matters.

As noted previously, however, the teaching staff as a whole was a diverse group within Jewish terms. It included some who were anti-religious, some who were very observant, and a great majority who did not live up to their Jewish "Way of Life" assumptions and were, in fact, very confused about their Jewishness themselves.

Because many of the teachers did not live in Apple River, the students could not observe the inconsistency in the teaching staff's instruction at school with their personal behavior after school hours. However, they were able to observe their teachers during school hours and they did observe them very closely during that time. In addition, there were periodic cracks in the teachers' adherence to the Jewish Way of Life assumption and it is not likely that those changes in posture went unnoticed. For instance, one teacher who did not keep kosher (observe the Jewish dietary laws) and who was obviously unconvinced of its value, doubtfully explained about keeping kosher to her students on a discussion on the subject, saying only that "We kill animals in a supposedly less inhumane way." Other teachers turned suddenly bored and unenthusiastic when faced with teaching the prayerbook and some teachers were remarkably able to "finish" the Bible curriculum before the end of the first half of the year.

It also could not have been hard for students to notice the teacher's aide with the transistor radio who periodically walked out of class on Sunday mornings to listen to the latest football information. One very senior teacher even left school early on certain Sundays in order to arrive at the football games before kickoff time. Students, too, were never far way when during recess teachers would excitedly describe the concert or movie they had been to on Friday evening, the Jewish Sabbath. Certainly they must have wondered why these self-proclaimed observant Jews were so uninterested in enforcing the rule to wear keepot (the Jewish skullcap), or why the teachers themselves frequently didn't even bother to wear them.

Interpersonal Relations and Teaching Methods

Students were also personally and intensely aware of the types of relationships that they were able to develop with their teachers. Even as some teachers (albeit, few) would try to describe the Biblical lesson of the importance and value of relationships between people, they would frequently shout angrily at their students in the following way:

> Steven, go sit in the corner. I don't want to see your face today. Sit there and shut up.
>
> If you can't keep quiet and behave like human beings, you are going to have to pay the price.

As the year progressed, the on-going "battles" between teachers and students grew fiercer and uglier. Constructive student comments and suggestions to their teachers about their learning experience were either ignored or openly discouraged. In one class students looked on horrified as one student finally began sobbing when the teacher continued to deny the boy's repeated requests to go to the bathroom. The teacher stated firmly to the student in front of the class: "There has not been one session that you haven't caused trouble!" Despite their teachers' behavior toward them, the students also heard their teachers speak both publicly and privately in disparaging tones about many other people, Jews and non-Jews alike. Depending on the teacher's personal ideological stance, there was either hostile criticism of orthodox Jews as being narrow-minded and isolationist, or smug mocking of reform Jews as not being really Jewish. The most severe and deep-felt anger and resentment, however, was left for the non-Jews, who frequently bore the brunt of religious jokes and were also the object of prejudiced comments.

What may have been the lack of instructional expertise among some of the teachers also seemed to provide problems for successful implementation of affective goals. Apparently without intent, teachers would sometimes set a mood in the class or exhibit an attitude that was different from what they desired. In attempting to teach some of the history of the holiday of Hanukah, one teacher lectured for two weeks prior to the holiday. She omitted all mention of the joy of Hanukah and denied any opportunity for celebration of what for many students was the raison d'etre for being Jewish. In addition, there was never any attempt to confront the Jewish identification crises students faced at this time of the year. (In private, even the rabbi and the principal spoke together of their own children's conflicts over not being able to participate in certain Christmas festivities.) Another area of recurring problems involved instruction during the elective period in which many classes were focused around music and arts and crafts. Several of the teachers in these classes were unable to integrate any Jewish theme or project with the technical aspects of their class, leaving many students to their own designs making wooden airplanes and drawing spacecraft. Due to the "doing" aspect of electives, the students' enthusiasm for them stood out sharply compared to other classes. However, the very limited inclusion of Jewish content in the electives tended to confuse the reason for that preference.

The Secondary Status of Jewish Learning and Jewish Life

Another factor affecting effective instruction was the attitude the students themselves brought to the classroom. Certainly it seemed that the parents of the students had an important impact on that attitude. Although the students could not observe their teachers' Jewish behavior, they were quite able to observe their parents' behavior and they were able to compare that with what their parents said about being Jewish and about Jewish behavior. What many of the students could observe was that the act of sending their children to Shalom School was their primary, and for some nearly only, Jewish behavior. They saw and they knew that regardless of what their parents said, the substance of the Jewish "Way of Life" assumption was not something that was part of their parents' lives.

The students' own world and lifestyle, of course, was not very different from their parents' in terms of a Jewish "Way of Life." Students came to Shalom School talking about sports, movies, spacecraft, and public school homework. For many of the students, Shalom School served as an interruption of activities that they would have preferred to have been involved in. Said one fourth grader to the researcher:

> Student: Did you say we could tell you what we liked and what we didn't like?
>
> Researcher: Yes
>
> Student: Well, this school interrupts everything. I could be dancing to my record album now, or decorating the house for Halloween.

During class the students' minds did not wander far from where their thoughts had been prior to class. In a session about Moses, one fifth grade boy excitedly raised his hand to speak, only to relate a vaguely related joke he had heard on the Hollywood Squares, a television program. In another class, during Hanukah, students unconsciously whistled and sang the tune "Jingle Bells" as they ran out to recess. In this same class, one of the most active participants in the fifth grade stood up, and walked to the researcher during the middle of class, handing him the following verse she had conceived that hour:

> Roses are reddish,
> Violets are bluish,
> If it wasn't Christmas,
> We'd all be Jewish.

In an incident at the beginning of the school year at the time of the Jewish New Year, a teacher asked his class about the "Shofar,"[9] a symbol of the holiday. "I know," answered one boy, "a chauffeur (sic) is the person who drives your car around."

Although the principal recognized at some level the culture gap that existed between staff and students, there was little that she felt able to do about it. She said:

I think all of us are out of touch with the suburban child, but I don't know how you can take a course in 'suburban child.' But it is something I plan to work on, getting to know these kids better—when I have time.

The extent to which she misunderstood "the suburban child" became clear when she suggested that students had not watched an historic event from Israel because it was televised on the Jewish Sabbath.[10] In actuality, several students had watched the historic event, but primarily for the reason that they had already turned on their TV sets to watch the Michigan-Ohio State football game, which at one point was pre-empted to cover the historic moment.[11]

As noted earlier, the effect of the part-timeness of the school, the social environment, and the general "loose" attitude towards Jewish schooling by staff and parents together was not lost upon the students. These factors, together with those described here, left the students with mostly confused images and feelings about being Jewish. At least some of those feelings were not overly difficult to ascertain. First, the students learned that while being Jewish had some value and held some importance, certainly enough for their parents to be willing to fight with them every week to attend, their experience at the school told them that its value relative to other activities and institutions, etc. was not so great. As such, they knew that Shalom School was important enough to attend, but not important enough to take seriously. Although that fact was acknowledged, it was not always easy for the children aged ten to thirteen to fully comprehend its import.

Secondly, students were being asked, in a sense, to distinguish between their feelings about Shalom School and their feelings about being Jewish. This was difficult, however, because for many of them Shalom School was the primary, if not singular, Jewish experience in their lives, and they disliked it. As one teacher warned:

If they hate it [Shalom School], they cannot feel strongly about being a Jew.

What the students were asked to do was to accept on the teacher's word the fact that there were positive and desirous elements of Jewish life and religion. These positive elements were presented by the teachers in highly vague terms, because they themselves did not more clearly understand or experience them. Thus it was difficult for the students to challenge that ultimate essence of Judaism that sounded so different from their school experience and which they never saw people practice or live out. Sometimes the concept of the State of Israel was used in this way, glorifying beyond all possible proportions a nation and experience that was out of reach for almost all students in order to maintain commitment and identification. Some students were able to make this distinction between Shalom School and being Jewish; others were not. Most, it seemed, identified strongly with a positive but very blurred vision of the Jewish people while feeling very confused about what it all meant and why their only experience in Jewish life was so negative. In this way, it seemed they did not have to deny their feelings from their own experience, yet they still could believe what their teachers told them.

Finally, despite the attempts of the school staff to convey a certain image and feeling about being Jewish through the affective curriculum, the students appeared to come away with an image and feeling about being Jewish that was not very different from their teachers' and parents'. The staff's desire to create some change and greater involvement in Jewish life through the school was not successful. What the students learned about being Jewish was vague and ambiguous, and the feelings they developed were marked by ambivalence. Indeed, that image was a more accurate representation of the true condition of the Jews of Apple River than the picture their teachers had unsuccessfully attempted to present in class.

Social Development

Parents looked to Shalom School as a place for their children to meet and be with other Jewish friends. They repeatedly stressed this interest to the researcher in written comments like these:

Enables opportunity to socialize with other Jewish children.

Have my children associate with other Jewish children since there are none in their public school.

Meeting other Jews.

Children being with other Jewish children.

The school staff also hoped that children at the school would make social contacts, however, most did not see this as part of the school's responsibility in programming or curricular development. In their minds, programming for social relations was the domain of other Jewish organizations. As a result, despite an air of informality and an initial friendly feeling about the school, the only formally structured time for social contact among students was recess.

Within the classroom, most instruction was in the form of lecture or individual assignment. Only in one class did a teacher structure group projects. This same teacher, too, took class time to celebrate students' birthdays, giving time for social interaction and facilitating such interaction through the organization of the celebrations.

The students enthusiastically welcomed such opportunities. Like their parents, the students cherished this brief chance for friendship with other Jewish children. For many, it was the only positively experienced aspect of Shalom School. Typical of their feelings were comments such as:

I like to come to see my friends.

I only come to see Allen.

The only reason I don't cut every week is because my friends are here.

During recess time, a major change that was easily observable came over most students. From a tired, forlorn, quick-tempered, and uninterested forebearance in the classroom burst forth energetic, happy, agreeable and excited children. Some gathered in large groups, others two by two, to play ball, write on the blackboard, or whisper about the opposite sex. Some students used the time to talk informally and work cooperatively with their teachers to whom they otherwise played adversary during class. Not only was recess the student's favorite period of school, but for most it was the only permissible time to interact directly with the other Jewish children.

The students, nevertheless, found other opportunities to interact as well. Although their circumstance was aided by teachers regularly arriving late to school, students developed clever mechanisms of delaying the start of class while enjoying their friends' company. They also learned how to extend recess time and classroom interruptions for additional social activity. Where most of their social interaction occurred, however, was during class and behind the teacher's back. In every classroom in the school, students employed a well-developed alternative communication system that included note passing, facial expression, whispering, soft talking, moving about, acting, and shouting.

Teachers interpreted most any action that was not between teacher and student to be a sign of misbehavior and a threat to their authority. Their reaction to student interaction was to eliminate it through verbal power, by splitting up groups, and by cancelling recess. Typical of the teacher's action was this threat, "If I separate you three again, I will never again let any of you sit together." The students, in turn, resented their teachers' interference in their social development and purposely intensified those behaviors that most irritated their teachers. In such a way, a never ending struggle developed.

By falsely assuming the well-being of the Jewish community and by modeling the Jewish school after the American public school, there was no opportunity for the pressing issue of Jewish social development to enter into the school curriculum. Nevertheless, the need for social contact with their Jewish peers was so dominant in the minds of parents and students that it forced itself into the school program, in however a disruptive manner that may have been. At the risk of scolding and chastisement by their teachers, and during the few recess minutes each day that the staff took a break from "teaching," the students got on with the business of what they perceived as one of the most important reasons for their being at school—developing a personal community of Jewish friends and identifying with the Jewish group.

The Classroom Experience

The focal point for all the effort in developing curricula, in organizing schedules, in struggling over finances, and in hiring teachers, etc., was the time that students and teachers met in their classes. However, just as well-intentioned preparation and optimistic hopes centered on those few hours, so, too, were the problems of identity and community dissolution unmistakably present in the classroom. What follows on the next few pages is a composite description of a typical day (Schoem, 1988a) at Shalom School:

After a day of work*, school, and/or study, the teachers gather to drive together to Shalom School. In their carpool, four tired teachers talk about and analyze their experiences at the school and also prepare themselves for the upcoming session. Their mood is one of frustration and anger and the tone of their comments range from sardonic humor to thoughtful resignation. One teacher reflects on his experience at the school, saying:

> I had some faith in it in September but I didn't realize how futile and frustrating it would be until I was here for a while. Within two weeks I realized I had made the mistake. If I made the commitment, though, I'm not going to break it...I have never worked with a more difficult group of kids in any setting. They are just a very wild, very rowdy, very hyperactive bunch of kids.

For the students, their day at public school blends into their afternoon at Shalom School. They feel tired from sitting in class all day only to have to rush to get to Shalom School on time. If they are lucky, they are able to get home for a very quick snack before they are driven to school. Some students do not think about what lies ahead for them in the afternoon school; others think about being with friends but being bored by both the content and instruction. Anticipating the approaching session that afternoon, one girl says:

> And no one listens. We just draw pictures and stuff and the teacher talks to himself. He knows what he's talking about but we don't.

Most students arrive at school between 3:55 and 4:05. School officially begins at 4:00. They talk and play among themselves, fantasizing about futuristic aircraft, remembering sports events, whispering and giggling about boys, girls, doing public school homework, or just wandering around the building. The teachers arrive in a rush by 4:10, apologizing to the principal and running to their classes.

---

*Reprinted from *Persistence and Flexibility: Anthropological Perspectives on the American Jewish Experience* by Walter Zenner, editor, by permission of the State University of New York Press. © 1988 State University of New York.

When the teacher arrives in his classroom, he finds his students relaxing in their chairs, most already bored in anticipation of the lesson to follow, a few feeling feisty and antagonistic, and a few ready to listen. Since the teacher has prepared for only half of the lesson time, he decides to use his other time to discuss a recent PLO raid into Israel. Shortly after he begins, about 4:15, the principal walks in, looking very harassed after another tense discussion with her administrative assistant. She gives the teacher flyers for the students announcing an event at the synagogue. The students begin to talk while the principal is there and their talk grows louder when she leaves.

The teacher attempts to begin his discussion again but is upset at noise and lack of interest. He warns the students that he takes this subject very seriously and will get very angry with them if they continue to joke about it. They continue to make jokes. At 4:20, the school board chairperson opens the door, smiles at the teacher, looks around the classroom, and then leaves. The students all turn around to watch her.

The teacher decides to change the focus of his discussion and asks the students what the word "Tzedakah" means to them. No one answers. The teacher begins lecturing on a related subject when one student finally raises her hand to answer the original question. "Oh yeah," she says, "You mean Neil Sedaka."

At 4:25 the teacher decides to begin the lesson that he has prepared on Siddur, the prayerbook. Although he thinks the subject is important, he is critical of the way he perceives that the administration wants him to teach it. He also is aware that the students do not find it interesting. Earlier, he has told the researcher:

> They expect you to teach the kids the prayers by heart. But the minute you bring the prayerbooks out, the kids turn off their interest.

Indeed, the class responds as expected. As he takes out the book, one boy appears to be sleeping, another is playing with his eraser, a third is stuck in a contorted position having tangled and twisted himself in his chair. During the course of the year parents and members of the administration made comments describing student behavior during class. Among them were the following:

> Kids walking on the table.
>
> Mocking the teacher's comments.
>
> Throwing paper airplanes.
>
> Intimidation and scapegoating kids till they cry.
>
> Interrupting discussions with rude comments.
>
> A jungle.

A Confusion of Purpose in the Classroom

> My daughter is afraid to go that class.
>
> If this is what goes on in a synagogue school, I just don't know what.
>
> What the kids have learned is that when you come to Hebrew school, you can misbehave.

At 4:35 another teacher walks in looking for books for her class. The two talk for a moment and she leaves empty-handed. At 4:38, a student comes in looking for his class. He is sent away. In the meantime, the rabbi, school board chairperson, and administrative assistant have gathered in a room where the principal is making a phone call. The following comment is made while they sit there:

> I think it is disturbing that a Hebrew school has discipline problems. It makes me sad. You would hope that we would be a different caliber of people. I think there's something basically wrong in the world. There's uncertainty. Expenses are very high. People may have to move because of their jobs. The rabbi is doing more and more counseling.

By 4:40, through insult, intimidation, and persistence, the teacher has finally quieted down his class. The students read the same prayer aloud, one by one. The teacher helps them with their many mistakes in reading the Hebrew. By 4:45 several questions regarding recess and the time have already been asked, and, after threatening to withhold recess, the teacher excuses his students at 4:50.

Recess gives students and teachers alike time to socialize and recuperate. Two teachers come by the classroom of the one being described. The teachers alternately speak (and complain) in Hebrew and English, using Hebrew exclusively when students walk by. One describes an unpleasant incident that occurred in her class that day. She is not happy with the support she has received from the principal and remarks:

> We've been trying to throw this person out for five weeks without any success. [the principal] couldn't even get the student to leave the room. If the principal doesn't get respect, then the teachers can't get respect.

The third teacher, nodding her head in agreement and support, adds a comment reflecting her own experience. She says: "I don't want to do this; why am I here?"

After recess, at 5 PM, the students return and the teacher begins to talk about a period of Jewish history. During the next half hour a wide range of what may be described as "bored behaviors" occur. The following list names the more common of these types of behavior that students do during class at Shalom School.

<u>Bored Behaviors</u>

1. Looking at a wristwatch
2. Playing with a wristwatch
3. Playing with anything in one's hand
4. Doodling
5. Making airplanes
6. Making paper footballs
7. Making other paper toys
8. Closing one's eyes
9. Moving chairs
10. Sniffing
11. Making weird noises
12. Looking out the window
13. Talking
14. Whispering
15. Passing Notes
16. Rocking on chairs
17. Kicking
18. Hitting
19. Staring into space
20. Tying shoes
21. Putting on clothing
22. Taking off clothing

After 5:15 students become very anxious about knowing the exact time, and questions about dismissal begin. By 5:25 many students have already closed their books and packed their school belongings. They then begin putting on their overcoats and at 5:30 are finally dismissed.

The researcher asked both students and parents to describe their perception of the typical day at Shalom School. The parents were able to give, at best, only a sentence or two of highly impressionistic, almost guessing, information. Two of the most detailed descriptions offered by students are presented below.

> A. You go in and find no one is in the classroom. This is at four o'clock. So you decide to walk around, find another kid or something. And then you get back and it's ten minutes late. And the teacher says, 'Why are you late?' But you were already there on time. And then you sit down and have a discussion about how if you are ever late again they will have to call your parents. But they never call the parents. And then usually the teacher reads something from a book. About twenty minutes into it, the recess questions begin. Then you go out for recess and come back a little late, same as before class. Class continues; people listen to what's worth listening to—either the teacher or a friend. I fool around with a pencil. And that goes on the rest of the day.

> B. We usually start fifteen minutes late and have a ten minute break. So we have only an hour really. Then with the first teacher we have these reports. I just copied it straight out of the book. Then sometimes we read in the Chumash [Torah]. And what good does that do? We don't understand it. And the teacher is just figuring out that we don't understand it. Then we have the rabbi and go over stuff for the Bar Mitzvah. But I already had mine so I talk with Janet who also had hers. The only time you learn is kindergarten to third grade.

In the daily classroom experience, the myriad of complex problems confronting the Jewish school came to life. What these problems created was a frustrating, almost debilitating experience that caused anger and conflict and was painful to face on a daily basis. From the deceptive assumptions about community and identity to the confused social and organizational structures, to the unrealistic program of curriculum and instruction, the chaotic experience at Shalom School seemed to metaphorically represent the outpouring of the anxious and deeply conflicted emotions of Jews in Apple River, confronting in their own lives the dilemma of being Jewish in a non-Jewish America.

Chapter Eight

ONE PEOPLE, MANY CONFLICTS

Staff and Students

Most students were forced by their parents to attend this non-compulsory institution. Unlike secondary schooling, attendance was a parental, not a state mandate. They found that the classroom instruction was foreign to their lives and, also, that it was often very boring. Some of the students also realized that they were being used as the instrument of their parents' tie with Jewish life. Regardless of whether their parents shared the Jewish Way of Life assumption, many students found their parents' inconsistent attitude and behavior in this regard to be hypocritical. Furthermore, the students recognized the low value placed on their Jewish schooling by their parents because it was seen as having no relation to their future success in college, professional life, and the material world. As a result of these factors, it seemed, these same students who were reported to be well disciplined and highly achievement oriented in public school acted in a disruptive, uninterested, and uncooperative manner at Shalom School.

Frustrated Together in the Classroom

The staff felt great frustration in their experience at Shalom School and blamed the parents of their students for the school failures (Schoem, 1979). However, the teachers had little or no contact with their students' parents and were most often unable to express their anger directly to them. On the other hand, the teachers did have twice weekly encounters with the uninterested and disruptive students. Although in many respects they sympathized with the students' position and their behavior, they felt forced to maintain an air of discipline in their classrooms and often found themselves in tense confrontations with them as a result. Over the course of the year, these confrontations, as well as their growing anger with the parents, created a hostile atmosphere between teachers and students, to the extent that the classroom became an emotional "battle zone."

Certain attitudes that the teachers brought with them to the school also seemed to inhibit the possibility of closer relations with all of their students. One teacher said:

> Of course, you always have the dumb ones who don't know what's flying at all... You can't let kids make up their own mind about how they think or feel about things.

Other negative attitudes towards students were picked up by new teachers from those more experienced. After a few months on the job, one new teacher stated with acceptance one of those new attitudes she had learned:

> I think with some of these kids—they're already pretty much written off.

At a staff orientation meeting prior to the start of the school year there was an attempt to approach the issue of disciplining students in humanistic terms. While it was openly acknowledged "that discipline was the big issue last year," the rabbi introduced the session as a discussion on "Human Beings and Classroom Control" and proceeded to instruct the teachers that "the people are your curriculum." However, that approach seemed to affect the rare teacher. The atmosphere in the classroom of one very young teacher, who never felt accepted as an equal even by the other teachers, stood out in the warmth and caring shown between teacher and student and among the students themselves. In another class that stood out because it was an exception to the rule, a teacher calmly yet forcefully settled down a student who was extremely angry and bitter at being forced to attend Shalom School. Their exchange went as follows:

> Teacher: That's the second time.
> Student: It's my father who brought me here.
> Teacher: When you are here, you must behave, Simon.
> Student: Oh, shut up.
> Teacher: Simon, just be quiet. Next time I will be angry.
> Student: You can't hit me.
> Teacher: I'm not going to hit you, but you can be angry from words.

Antagonism, Hostility, and Distance

What was more typical of student-teacher interaction, particularly as the year progressed, was antagonism, separation, and hostility. Even on the very first day of school, the principal set this tone when she decided to meet with her teachers in a classroom for a few moments prior to class. In the classroom several anxious ten year olds sat quietly at their tables with new notebooks and pencils awaiting their teacher. Without any direct recognition of the students, the principal stated loudly and sharply for all those present to hear, "We have to chase the kids out of that room!" Mimicking and surpassing the principal's sharp tones, a few teachers started in by shouting the nervous and confused students out of the room.

In place of a teacher who was fired/resigned after the first two weeks, the principal showed her priorities by choosing an inexperienced Israeli teacher who was described in glowing terms for having good classroom control skills because he had just come to the U.S. after serving in a well known, crack Israeli army unit. Highly enthusiastic about her selection, the principal showered praise on his quality as a teacher, strictly for his ability to discipline, at the next school board meeting:

He had the class under control. He talked continuously and the kids didn't know what hit them.

In addition to emphasizing control and power in their verbal communication with their students, the teachers also increasingly separated themselves from their students and withdrew from student contact and interaction. Whereas they initially joked and played with students at recess and before school, over time they spoke only with other staff and in Hebrew, so students couldn't understand. Similarly, the high school student aides, following the example of the teachers, grew more verbally abusive, hostile, and separated from the students during the course of the year.

Different teachers in grades four through seven acted and spoke with their students in different manners. One teacher was closed, tight, and demanding; another was loud and threatening; a third was sarcastic; and a fourth was intimidating in her attempt to be cold and emotionless. Another teacher attempted to reason with students on a high intellectual level and, finally, one teacher tried to calmly and honestly present herself to students, sometimes according to their parents' degree of support for the teachers. In a different way, the teachers perceived an administrative reluctance or inability to discipline children of influential synagogue board members. One said:

> We could do anything we want except take disciplinary measures. That is, except with kids whose parents are active in the synagogue.

The principal confirmed, at least, that she herself felt pressure from above, saying:

> It is difficult when the school has to deal with people who are higher-ups in the synagogue.

As the year progressed, the following kinds of comments, expressed in tones in accord with the various descriptions of the types of teacher interaction listed above, became more and more commonplace.

A. Teacher: Boy, are you guys lazy.
Class: giggles [nervously]
Teacher: That's not a joke.

B. Hands down and ears open when somebody speaks.

C. No questions

D. Teacher to other teachers: I have all the monsters together today because Ron is absent. But I have my whip out.

E. Do we have to go over every lesson four times?

F. The reason I'm giving you all these names is in case when you're older someone comes up to you and mentions these names, you won't go, Duh!

G. Someone has interrupted me. His name is Mike and he is one of my worst students. I want to announce that anyone who disrupts will be kicked out.

H. I had a talk with you before you came into class—remember it!

Some teachers' respect for their students even dropped to a point of personal dislike, distrust, and disregard. One bitter teacher commented:

What I teach is the values that these kids lack and normal human beings have.

Another teacher, who eventually left her teaching job because of the ugly interaction with her students, described how her relationship with them had deteriorated.

I began to hate my students. They were cruel and hostile, snobbish, materialistic, and a very nasty bunch. I finally felt no sympathy for them and I couldn't reach beyond that. I could have handled them, but I didn't like them.

The students, for their part, did little to ameliorate the situation. In a pattern not unlike that of the teachers', a growing number of students over the course of the year intensified their own disruptive and antagonistic behavior in class and toward their teachers. In addition to the structural conditions that put them into Shalom School in the first place, the students rebelled at what they experienced as day-to-day abuses, put-downs, and boredom, and also struggled for their share of power in the classroom. One particularly independent and disruptive student remarked cooly:

Why I'm really acting off? I had my Bar Mitzvah already and it really doesn't matter anymore. And there's no way they can force me to go after this year... Sometimes I feel like getting the teacher; sometimes I feel good. Hebrew school is stupid. It is fucked.

Another self-proclaimed disruptive student carefully analyzed the student-teacher relationship at Shalom School in less emotional terms. Suggesting that the problem had little to do with individual personalities of teachers or students, she said:

And the teachers—yeah. They are terrible. To me it seems the only reason they're here is for the money. But even from the good teachers you can't learn anything because we're so used to goofing off and doing what we want that we tell the teacher what to do. And then we get a super strict teacher and we're just not used to that. When that happens, we say 'whoa'! But, I guess no matter what a Hebrew teacher does, they can't be right.

One People, Many Conflicts

Throughout the year, teachers and students fought pitched battles with an ever decreasing number of peaceful interludes. While the combatants risked and sustained heavy and sometimes critical emotional casualties, there was little that either group could have won. Any sense of Jewish community that existed and any suggestion of the existence of Jewish ethics in human relations appeared to be the ultimate victims of the struggle at every class meeting. While at infrequent and detached moments some faculty and a few of the older students could see the futility and destructiveness of their interaction, the emotional intensity of the classroom and the structure and circumstances of the school's operation itself did not allow for any reconciliation of the parties involved or for resolution of the conflict.

Parents and Staff

Despite the transcending presence of the Jewish Way of Life assumption within the school, most of the parents who sent their children to Shalom School did not share that assumption. Furthermore, even among those who did, there was often sharp disagreement.

Three Subgroups in the School

In regard to these disagreements, the adults of Shalom School, including both parents and staff, were best understood as comprising three groups (see below). Group A was primarily comprised of the staff of the school but also included a small number of parents, usually drawing from those sitting on the school board. This group shared the Jewish Way of Life assumption and also was actively involved in the school. Group B consisted primarily of parents who shared the Jewish Way of Life assumption and took an active interest in the school. It also included a smaller number of parents who viewed Judaism as an important but clearly peripheral part of their lives. Finally, Group C was primarily made up of the largest group of parents, which included those for whom Judaism played only a peripheral role in their lives and who only took a passing interest in the school. In addition, it included a small number of parents more similar to the majority of Group B.

<u>Group A</u>
Primary Representation
   Characteristics

1. Staff
   - Jewish way of Life Assumption
   - Active involvement in school

Secondary Representation
   Characteristics

2. Parents
   - Jewish Way of Life Assumption
   - Active involvement in school

<u>Group B</u>
Primary Representation
  Characteristics

1. Parents
   - Jewish Way of Life Assumption
   - Active interest in school

Secondary Representation
  Characteristics

2. Parents
   - Peripheral involvement in Jewish Way of Life
   - Passive interest in school

<u>Group C</u>
Primary Representation
  Characteristics

1. Parents
   - Peripheral involvement in Jewish Way of Life
   - Passive interest in school

Secondary Representation
  Characteristics

2. Parents
   - Jewish Way of Life Assumption
   - Active interest in school

As the school year progressed, Group A and Group B became increasingly opposed to one another despite their shared assumption. The people of Group A perceived the parents of Groups B and C as representing one large entity, uninterested either in things Jewish or in the school. There was never a recognition of the different attitudes of parents in Groups B and C. The position taken by Group A was almost always according to staff interests, and as a result, there was even distrust between the staff and parents within Group A.

The people of Group A felt that the parents of Shalom School had a responsibility to be involved Jewishly in a personal way in their homes if they were going to send their children to a Jewish school. One school board member distinguished the parents in her own mind simply as "Those who care and those who don't care." To her, those who didn't care represented Groups B and C and she had expressed no interest in planning the school around those people's interests. She felt strongly that parents who didn't come to school board meetings, were indicating that the school "obviously doesn't mean that much to them." One teacher, who was very resentful of the parents, expressed his perception of their attitude toward the Jewish school, saying:

> Parents don't want kids to become any more Jewish. They want them to be American. By sending their kids to Sunday school, they don't have to do anything at home. By taking the most diluted form of Jewish training and sending their kids, they feel they don't have to do anything else because they have fulfilled their responsibility.

Another teacher revealed her anger in questioning why the parents sent their children to Shalom School at all. She said:

Why should the kids have to go to Hebrew school and then return home and find a Christmas tree in their home. It's hypocritical!

The parents of Group B were as self-deceptive as the people of Group A in their assumptions about their own Jewish Way of Life. However, they deeply resented the accusation that they were neither adequately Jewish or fulfilling their Jewish responsibility to their children within their own homes. They also resented the implication that their attitudes and behavior were the cause of any problems in the school. As one parent defensively stated:

I think the school expects us to encourage our children to have a positive attitude—which we do.

The parents of Group B, in the meantime, grew tired and irritated at their children's constant complaints about the school and wondered whether the problems of the school might not be solved with a more dedicated, better trained, and different staff.

The parents of Group C were more realistic about their Jewish attitudes and behavior and did not share in the Jewish Way of Life assumption. Although they wanted to retain for themselves and their children an identification with the Jewish people and religion, they were not particularly interested in the affairs of the school beyond their children's regular attendance. As one of many satisfied parents in Group C stated:

I don't really know what it is going on there, but I have gotten positive reports. We rely on the school to keep us posted if there is a problem; but I'm not gonna look for work.

It was interesting to note that while the parents of Group C in many ways matched the "negative" descriptions that made the people in Group C so resentful, the parents of Group C were certainly the most satisfied people in the school. Also, while the people of Group A were critical of what they perceived as deception and hypocrisy among the parents of Groups B and C, they did not perceive any inconsistencies in their own assumptions, thoughts, and behavior. Finally, the parents of Group B, who were similar in many ways to the people of Group A except for not translating their interest into involvement at the school, assessed the problems at the school not in terms of commitment or practice of things Jewish as Group A had done, rather they saw the problems as being "school" problems which were not related to the home environment of school families and which could best be solved through teaching and administrative staff changes.

Socio-Economic Differences Between Parents and Staff

Another factor serving to separate staff and parents was the matter of socio-economic differences. Most of the teachers in grades four through seven lived outside of Apple River near Collegetown, home of a large, prestigious university. Not only did the physical distance keep staff and parents apart, but there were much different social and cultural norms between Collegetown and Apple River. In defending their right to be different, one parent of Group A revealed some of what others in Apple River found objectionable:

> Now, I'm a liberal minded person and I have no problem with _____ [Collegetown] types. And as role models, I have no problems with the teachers. They're unique people; they're a little weird; but they're neat people. And I think some people who are more limited and closed-minded may object to them, that is, when I think of their sandals and beard—their appearance.

The differences in social norms were related to economic differences, too. The teachers were only in the very first stages of their professional careers, some working part-time at other jobs as well as at Shalom School, and others still pursuing university studies. Relative to the status of the teachers, the parents of Shalom School were much more established in their professions, and were earning enough money to live according to upper middle-class suburban standards.

The teachers perceived that the parents had substituted their interest in things Jewish with a love for and pursuit of material possessions. The teachers also found it difficult to work for people with such a higher standard of living. Finally, they disliked the fact that status, among the parents of Shalom School, seemed to be determined according to monetary wealth. One teacher ruefully remarked, "It's really money that counts here." Since they believed that their own role as teachers, which to them meant passing on the great tradition of the Jewish people in order to preserve the group for generations to come, was a revered position in Jewish history, they felt terribly resentful that among the people of Shalom School, they counted for very little. One teacher described her perception of her status among the parents of Shalom School as follows:

> They have no respect for us whatsoever. What would you think? The average parent looks with the same contempt at a Hebrew school teacher as they would with a grade school or high school teacher. In a community such as _____ [Apple River], where status values are firmly connected with financial success, this is a job for schmucks. And the kids know it, too. I mean, it's absolutely beyond them that we could be anything besides Hebrew school teachers.

The parents, in turn, while never acting to make the Collegetown teachers feel any more comfortable in Apple River or as part of the Shalom Synagogue community, were extremely unhappy with teachers who publicly noted the socio-economic stratification. Their impression was not that Collegetown teachers were jealous of their socio-economic status but rather that they looked negatively upon the Apple River adults and children in terms of culture and values just because of their greater wealth. Furthermore, the parents felt that letting socioeconomic differences have an effect on classroom instruction was improper and was a sign of unprofessionalism. At the open school meeting at the end of the year, one parent made this point:

> I don't care if teachers from _____ [Collegetown] think kids in suburbia are an abomination—that's their problem, not ours. But it shouldn't come into the class!

Growing Frustration and "Blaming"

By the middle of November, the students' disruptive behavior had grown to proportions that made it difficult for teachers to teach as they would have liked. The parents, at the same time, had grown tired of listening to their children's complaints about the school. There was a general consensus that all was not right in the school. At this point in time, the lines between Groups A and B were becoming defined. During recess, following parent visitation to the class one Sunday morning in November, a few parents gathered to talk with the teacher and principal. At the moment one rather upset mother began speaking by saying, "Frankly, I was bored," the principal and another parent who happened to be on the school board rapidly "answered" whatever she had to say until she gave up talking. The teacher, meanwhile, whispered to the researcher when the others had left, "Did you hear that parent? I am not going to let parents tell me how to teach!"

As the school year progressed and classroom problems only increased, the conflict, too, grew more intense. The staff became increasingly frustrated and resentful—some resigned; the parents became angrier and some demanded that certain staff not be rehired. Ugly gossip and rumors were whispered about. One teacher, the object of severe parental criticism, angrily described her experience and her bitter feelings:

> ...the mother, who hadn't talked to me all year, wants me fired. And _____ [the school board chairperson] agrees with her. Meanwhile, the rabbi and _____ [the principal] are telling me I'm doing a great job... Everything goes on behind your back. That's probably why the whole synagogue, the whole community is decaying... It should start at home and it doesn't. The parents don't spend enough time with their kids in general. But the parents in this community just think they can spend their money and pay for something and everything will be okay.

Another teacher, who had survived a similar experience a few years earlier, recalled her bout at the school:

> There's a lot of talking behind people's backs—distrust. There's not a lot of open, direct communication. My first year one of the teachers tried to gather parents against me to fire me. They never came to my class, or spoke to me (pause)—It was really bad... There is a lot of mouthing off by parents and high expectations, but they're not willing to do anything at home. The kids get double messages at home. Go to Hebrew school but don't bring it home.

By mid-year many of the teachers felt enormous pressure from the parents of their schoolchildren. While at least some of the pressure was more imagined than actual, that pressure was felt as being very real. Furthermore, without receiving any supportive feedback from the parents to contradict their perceptions, the teachers became more defensive of their own capabilities and increasingly critical of the parents' role. Said one teacher:

> They expect more from the teachers. They expect everything from the school and teacher. If there is a problem at school, it is teacher, not child's fault. The parents do nothing at home.

Another distraught teacher echoed similar sentiments, saying:

> If Judaism is positive at home and happens at home, school will have meaning. If a child learns esoterically about Havdalah at school but never experiences it—what does he need it for?!?

Certainly not all of the teachers' pressured feeling was imagined. The parents in Group B were highly critical of school affairs and placed the blame for school problems directly on the staffs' shoulders. One type of criticism implied a lack of dedication and commitment, as well as incompetence as the following parent suggested:

> Teachers in the public school district here want to teach here because the students are so bright; the pay here is one of the lowest in the state. So I feel if you have a born teacher, it won't matter how much we pay. And the same goes for the administrator.

Another parent criticized the staff for having too much professional pride to the point of inhibiting quality teaching. She even added that the reason for lack of greater parental involvement and participation in the school resulted from lack of interest and discouragement on the part of staff:

> Teachers here are very proud—the rabbi, too—they don't want to ask for help. They just want to do it their way. I think they are too proud and ashamed to ask the parents for help... As far as I see it, they don't want the parents too involved.

A third and major criticism had to do with the staff's inability to effect greater control and discipline in the school. Suggesting that this was the reason for his daughter not learning more at Shalom School, one parent said:

> If the Hebrew school operated more like a public school, if there were more discipline or order, she would be learning more. And I've heard it's been worse in the past.

Finally, as matters only continued to worsen, certain teachers were accused by some parents of becoming physically abusive with their students. Although such behavior was never observed by the researcher, one parent angrily confronted the principal and school board chairperson at the open school meeting at the end of the year, shouting:

> And the teachers shouldn't abuse the children. Last week a teacher threw chalk at the students.

As troubling incidents occurred, new criticisms were made, and imagined confrontations took place, the level of enmity and separation between Groups A and B escalated. By the spring months, the teachers became more outspoken in their belief that they alone were responsible for the entire burden of transmitting Jewish culture to the children of Apple River. Given their perception of the nature of the parents of Apple River, however, the teachers now felt, too, that their responsibility was an impossible task to fulfill. Two teachers commented:

> They feel that you're doing something so they don't have to do it. And if you didn't do it, then their kids just wouldn't learn.

> If I could change the community, I would. But if I were to change the school, and the community was the same, I don't think the school could be very different.

"Blaming" became one of the most common activities among the people in Groups A and B. Throughout the conflict and debate, parents in Group B considered the issue to be a school problem, and from their experience in the public schools, these people felt they knew how to handle school problems. The people in Group A saw the problem as being an overwhelming desire of parents in Groups B and C to assimilate to things "American." Of themselves, the people of Group A did not recognize their own deceptive assumptions and struggle in trying to live with integrity in two cultural worlds. Instead of confronting their common conflicts and dilemmas together (Schoem 1984B), the parents and staff of Shalom School became embroiled in a debilitating struggle with one another, only adding to the many problems and frustrations already facing the school.

A Glimpse at Other Relationships

Parents and Students

It was not within the scope of this research to directly observe parent-child interaction except in isolated situations. Furthermore, data gathered through interviews and informal discussion was limited to their relationship regarding Jewish schooling. The parents' interest in the school, as discussed earlier, did not in many cases extend beyond the act of sending their children to the school. The students, in turn, were resentful of having to miss free play time or after-public school activities for the Shalom School program whose intrinsic and material worth was clearly limited in their parents' minds and whose program of instruction they found boring. Also, the students found it confusing and hypocritical that the instruction at the school would not only be about a way of life foreign to their own lives, but it was a way of life that they were expected not to bring home, except perhaps in unobtrusive bits and pieces. In addition, while they enjoyed being with their Jewish peers at the school, most of their direct contact with them had to be conducted in a subversive manner.

The parents, as a rule, did not take their children's complaints about the school seriously. Either they assumed that it was just natural for students to complain about (Jewish) schooling, or they took the position that the opinion of young people was not worth listening to. This opinion was easy to accept because the students seemed powerless to back what they said. One father commented on this position, saying:

> I don't usually listen to kids because they see things from a different point of view.

Furthermore, the parents of Group C did not want to be involved with problems at Shalom School and did not care to be bothered by hearing about them.

The students, while not having any recognized power, were still able to effectively make themselves heard. In the classroom, the students' disruptive behavior and lack of interest and participation caused the teachers to react to them, although not always in the manner students would have preferred. The teachers perceived the students' behavior either as a reflection of their Jewishly deprived home backgrounds or as the result of simply being spoiled and bad children. They, in turn, either thrust greater anger and resentment at the parents of the students or became stricter disciplinarians and more personally hostile towards the students themselves. In the home, the students' level of complaints eventually reached a point that was unbearable to the parents of Group B. While they didn't necessarily listen to the content of their children's complaints, they did finally acknowledge and respond to the persistence and intensity of their protests. The parental reaction of Group B, however, did not take into consideration the fact that the problems at the school could have had anything to do with their own or their children's attitudes or behavior; rather, they demanded that the school staff make the necessary changes within the confines of the classroom that would soften their children's rebelliousness.

The Principal and the Staff and Congregation

The principal was the focal point for discussion and disagreement about the school as she was the most well-known and most central figure there. In addition to the other difficulties she experienced as administrator of the school, her professional relationships with the various interest groups in the school and synagogue were often tense, conflicted, and uncertain. In a non-professional capacity, people almost always said they liked her. However, there were few occasions when she and others met on that basis.

On a personal level, the principal associated herself more closely with members of the staff. She not only lived and shared in the cultural milieu of Collegetown, but economically she was far more on a par with her staff than with the Shalom Synagogue members. In addition, as a trained teacher, she understood personally the difficulties of classroom teaching and empathized with her staff in that respect. Finally, she shared with them the antagonism held against the parents of Groups B and C, and also blamed them for the schools' problems.

Although the faculty reported that they enjoyed being with the principal during relaxed moments, those were infrequent occurrences. In fact, her busy schedule and harried demeanor made them feel uncomfortable about approaching her at all most of the time. They distanced themselves from her as well because of the power she held over them in the hierarchical structure even though they did feel trusting towards her. However, they were cautious in their trust because of her seemingly very close ties with the school board and rabbi towards whom they felt considerably less trust.

Although there was respect and philosophical agreement between the principal and school board, tension and suspicions arose during the year over the questions of whether to appoint a full-time principal and whether the current principal should be re-hired as the full-time person. While the school board always publicly defended the current principal to parents and the congregational board, the question of her re-hiring caused some internal evaluative thinking and doubting within the school board itself. The principal felt that it was her strong efforts in the past years that had created the need, in a positive sense, for a full-time principal. To suggest that she either wasn't sufficiently competent, educated and certified, or simply worth the extra money involved, was to her a slap in the face. She was further hurt, even humiliated, when asked to formally apply for the new position by submitting a letter and resume and having to interview before a committee.

Despite her anxiety at the school board's sign of ambivalence, she recognized that they were her greatest supporters in the synagogue. She also felt very close and trusting of the rabbi. Most of her anger, therefore, was directed at the parents of Group B, who demanded a more open and serious search for a new principal. Some of these parents were also openly critical of the present principal and campaigned not to have her rehired. The large group of parents in Group C were generally satisfied both with the school and the principal. Those in that group who had contact with her reported positive reactions and those who did not have contact with her still had favorable impressions. This large group, however, which was typically not active in school affairs, also did not involve itself in this case to support the principal in her effort to be rehired.

Shalom School and Non-Affiliated Jews

Despite the conflicts among groups in the school regarding their perceived Jewish commitment and behavior, all those who chose to send their children to a

Jewish school and to become members of the synagogue constituted a select group among the Jewish people. According to the National Jewish Population Study (Maslow 1974:14) 58.2% of all Jews in the U.S. were reported to be "not at all active" in any Jewish organizations. An estimated 50-55% of Jews living in the greater metropolitan area including Apple River were not known to be members of any synagogue and did not send their children to any Jewish school (Massarik 1970). These Jews were defacto forgotten by the Jewish school because of its requirement for synagogue membership and because of its lack of educational outreach. While some school parents indicated that they had personal friends in this category of people, there was never any organized effort to make contact with these people.

In one situation after another, the unchallenged issues facing these groups of Jewish people created unbearable conditions. Their misunderstanding or inability to even recognize the commonality of their own dilemmas and struggles as Jews led to unnecessary conflict, bad feelings, and failure in the school. These problems then gained their own momentum, escalated and intensified, and created new and more difficult problems that in turn only further obscured the underlying problems.

Chapter Nine

SUCCESS IN THE SHORT-TERM: SURVIVAL AND IDENTIFICATION

The very fact of the school's existence and people's association with it, irrespective of its substance and content, was of considerable significance. Despite the problems present at Shalom School, there were a number of important, positive effects resulting from association with the school. (Schoem 1983B)

The Parents, The Family, and Judaism

The Shalom School served an important role in the Jewish identification of not only the students but also the parents of the students at the Shalom School. Whether it was more important or equal in importance to the role it played in the students' Jewish identification was difficult to ascertain. Yet the school functioned usefully in this regard, although mostly unknowingly and unintentionally.

Fulfilling Jewish Responsibility

The existence of the Shalom School gave parents an opportunity to send their children to Jewish school. Indeed, for most parents this was an important act. It signified, in some sense, a personal reaffirmation of the Israelites' covenant with God in their fulfillment of the responsibility "And you shall teach it to your children" (Deuteronomy 6:7). It also marked an historic tie with generations of Jewish parents who had in their own way and circumstances taken responsibility for their children's Jewish education through the centuries of time. It also, more immediately, satisfied the hopes and dreams of their own parents that their grandchildren would have the opportunity of a Jewish education and an exposure to the heritage of the Jewish people. Furthermore, it marked the attempt on their own part to ensure that their concerns for their children's well-being as Jews would be taken care of.

Although some parents and teachers did not consider the mere act of sending one's children to Shalom School a fulfillment of one's Jewish responsibility as a parent, it did represent to all at least some measure towards fulfilling that responsibility. Indeed, certain parents experienced a sense of guilt that they were only sending their children to the school and doing little else Jewishly. One such parent said:

> I am living as Jewish as I like yet I feel a certain pull for Shosh's education that we do a little more. I don't want to do anymore, but at times I feel we should.

Other parents felt quite satisfied that in just having their children attend the school they were taking a significant step. To many parents, their alternative would not have been to do any more Jewishly for their children but, rather, not to have even sent their children to the Shalom School. This group of parents were pleased with themselves for what they were doing, and thankful that the Shalom School existed so that they had the opportunity to do so. Citing community studies by Sklare (1967) and Gans (1956), Bock (1977) reports that this dynamic has been observed elsewhere. He writes:

> Both Sklare and Gans observe that Jewish education—specifically the organization of congregationally-run afternoon schools—is a mechanism for parents to believe they are passing on their values to their children when, in fact, they were responding to the dilemmas of their own identity.

The expectations of one parent, who felt directly responsible and proud for his child's education through the school, were not unlike those of many other parents:

> It's hard on the kids to grow up in a Christian world. I have a neighbor who thinks my kids are deprived because they don't get a gift on Christmas morning. Well, if I can help my child adjust to that kind of thing I'll be doing alright.

Parental Involvement

In addition to acting as an outlet for at least some fulfillment of parental responsibility, the school, also unsuspectingly, required that parents be actively involved in the daily routine of the school. Because of the distances involved in suburban living, it was necessary that parents take responsibility for their children's transportation to and from school each day. Although in some respects this activity seemed frivolous relative to the instructional program of the school, it provided for many parents the only Jewish activity that they performed on a routine basis. Not only was this "chauffeur ritual" routinely attended to, but for some parents it came at the expense of sacrificing time that could have been spent on other responsibilities or self-indulgent activities. In light of the dearth of Jewish behavior evident among the Shalom School parents, the "chauffeur ritual" took on a significance far beyond the frivolity that it might have otherwise appeared.

Secondly, some parents experienced a perceived strain on their family budget as a result of the costs of school tuition and synagogue membership dues. In a community where material concerns seemed so predominant, the allocation of monies for Jewish schooling represented for some parents a degree of strength in commitment that was otherwise not displayed during the year.

Bringing Judaism into the Home

In yet another unrecognized respect, the unhappiness of students and parents with their experience at Shalom School forced an issue of Jewish substance into their homes. Even in families where the parents would not discuss or recognize their children's complaints, the issue of Jewish schooling was raised and heard in the household. While it is not being suggested that the issue of Jewish schooling took up a significant portion of time or energy in the home, it did at the very least add an additional cause for families to "step out" of their routine to think about a Jewish subject. Further, as an additional Jewish factor in their lives, it was one that the children made very personal and immediate, unlike much of their institutional and distanced contacts with other Jewish affairs.

In a more positive and hoped for effect of the school, a smaller number of parents used their children's attendance there as a way of educating and/or easing themselves into a closer relationship with Jewish life. A couple of students told the researcher that they were sent to Shalom School so that they could learn enough to teach their parents at home. Other parents attended the infrequently held "parent education" classes while their children were at Shalom School on Sunday mornings. There was a certain group of parents, too, who either had always felt uncomfortable in the synagogue or who had in recent years drifted away from their synagogue and observational ties to Judaism. These parents welcomed their perceived new opportunity to come closer to Jewish life under the guise of introducing their children to synagogue activities, services, etc. The parents in this group did not represent a large percentage of the parents of Shalom School; nonetheless, some of them were thrilled with their new or renewed Jewish ties. One couple expressed this attitude with elation:

> We have been pulled into it. The more the children have been going, the more we have been pulled into it... We have become wholeheartedly swept into this.

The Synagogue

The synagogue itself clearly benefited from having Shalom School a part of it. Although the question remains whether the synagogue might have found other ways of attracting equal numbers of members without a school, in the context of the observed situation the school was a very important factor, sometimes the only one, that many people alluded to in discussing their decision to join the synagogue.

Membership, Money, and Status

The rabbi of the synagogue estimated that 35% of the synagogue membership had joined solely because of the membership requirement for attendance at the school. It was difficult to estimate the validity of his guess, given the complex nature of people's ties with Jewish life. The usual pattern that parents described in their path to synagogue affiliation was 1) a period without interest in Jewish life extending from one's Bar/Bat Mitzvah until the birth of one's children, 2) a recalling of parental affiliation with a synagogue as a child, and 3) the coming of school age for their children. At the time their children did reach school age, the parents made a decision that they wanted their children to be sufficiently educated for a Bar/Bat Mitzvah. Either immediately or in the next few years, the parents enrolled their children in Jewish school and joined the synagogue. Sklare (1967) indicates that parents with elementary school aged children were more than four times as likely to be affiliated with a congregation than parents with pre-school aged children.

Many parents openly discussed and understood the reason for required synagogue membership as being an insurance policy to maintain and increase the level of membership. One parent explained:

> They force you to join because they are afraid there wouldn't be enough members otherwise.

The rabbi reported that most members retained their affiliation, however, even after their children had graduated from the school. He inferred from this that regardless of their initial reason for affiliation, they had come to realize the benefits outside of schooling that warranted their remaining as members. While there may have been other reasons as well for the high retention rate, such as social pressure, and force of habit, guilt, and symbolic identification, it was not within the scope of this research to investigate that matter.

It was open to question, however, whether the membership requirement may have actually limited the number of students who attended the school. While the researcher did not question non-synagogue members in Apple River, some members reported that their friends in that category of people did not send their children to Jewish school precisely because of the cost. Although it appeared that people living in these suburban towns were not unable to afford the cost of membership, it did seem that they were unwilling to allocate that amount of money towards such an endeavor. In addition, the synagogue did provide a sliding membership scale for those whose income was below a certain level. In general, however, it seemed that the synagogue's membership requirement for Shalom School had the effect of burgeoning the membership files at the risk of limiting school enrollment.

The attraction of members to the synagogue benefited it in at least two ways. Financially, the synagogue accrued a considerable income from membership even after accounting for its annual financial support of the school. The synagogue also received income from appeals for additional individual donations. With more members from whom to seek donations, the amount of that source of income was likely to increase. Furthermore, as the financial status and possessions of the synagogue grew, as did the number of members in the synagogue, it was expected that the synagogue's stature in the "institutional Jewish community" would grow. Certainly the validity of this expectation had been upheld since Shalom Syna-

Success in the Short-Term: Survival and Identification 125

gogue's original inception as a small outpost on the suburban frontier. Also, with an enlarged membership, the opportunity of attracting "important" personalities either in the secular or Jewish community, increased. Finally, with more funds and more people, the synagogue was able to develop its programs, improve its physical structures, and anticipate greater numbers of people participating in all activities. In this respect, parents who had become members only because of the school connection were influenced in yet another Jewish connection, that of Jewish social development. In Bock's words (1977:23):

> Schooling and other educational experiences may result in social contacts—(as well as in learning) if not always for the younger generation, then sometimes for their parents.

The Students and Jewish Identification

To many of the parents and staff, the anticipated effect of their children's Jewish schooling was not expected to show up for many years, probably until adulthood. One parent explained this attitude to the researcher in terms of what he called "the Vegetable Theory:"

> Just like little kids don't like veggies but do like them when they become adults; so it is with Hebrew school. You have to go when you're young even though you don't like it.

The rabbi often commented that even though superficial appearances sometimes indicated that students had not learned values that the school taught, those indicators were misleading because of the students' inability to articulate their values. Other parents agreed with the rabbi, even though at their age they themselves were apparently still unable to "articulate" their own Jewish values. One parent estimated that the value of Jewish schooling is not realized until one is twenty to twenty-five years old and in search of identity. It's "important for later," said another parent. "Marcy will appreciate it later."

Among those who looked to the future to see the effects of Jewish schooling, there was an acceptance of the fact that the ultimate results might be slow in coming. As one mother stated:

> [Their] tie to Judaism may not show up for ten years, but that's okay.

Some parents, like the chairperson of the school board, accepted the idea of this kind of "delayed reaction" to Jewish schooling because of changes in attitudes toward Judaism over the years that they had witnessed in themselves. Said the chairperson:

> When I was a young person, I hated Hebrew school, but when I was an adult, I felt comfortable when I went to the synagogue.

Finally, even a few of the students took on the assumption of future rewards from Jewish school. One boy said:

See, I don't really like to come because I have softball, basketball, and karate at public school after school, and sometimes I have soccer. But I figure that this will help me later on. I read this article that if you don't have any religion you'll feel pretty insecure.

Important Short-Term Effect

In the last decade, several studies (see especially Dashefsky and Shapiro 1974; Himmelfarb 1974; Bock 1977) have examined the validity of the assumption of the long-range effectiveness of Jewish schooling. Their results have provided some encouragement for the potential of Jewish schooling but have provided an even greater discouragement for the schools as they are presently constituted. Reviewing four studies on this subject (Laserwitz 1973; Cohen 1974; Dashefsky and Shapiro 1974; Himmelfarb 1974), Himmelfarb (1975:3) concluded that "The more Jewish schooling one receives, the more likely it is that the person will be an adult who identifies Jewishly or is religiously involved." However, Himmelfarb notes that the data indicates that most students in Jewish supplementary schools do not attend for a sufficient number of hours to effect any greater impact on adult religious involvement "beyond the level obtained by those with no Jewish schooling." Summarizing, he writes:

> According to the data, at least 3,000 hours of religious instruction are needed before Jewish schooling has any lasting impact. Very few Jewish students get that much religious schooling. **Thus in terms of long range consequences for Jewish identity, these data indicate that the type of Jewish education received by over 80% of those American Jews who have received any Jewish education has been a waste of time.** [Emphasis added]

Perhaps the strong interest in long-term effect persists as a result of the scarcity and inadequacy of Jewish education for adults. Nevertheless, it was only within the scope of this study to observe more immediate effects, and despite a lack of statistical controls, there were repeated incidents, explanations, and attributions that caused the researcher to consider the possibility of an important immediate effect of Shalom School for its students in terms of Jewish identification. Thus, despite the gloomy conclusions regarding the long-range effect of supplementary Jewish schooling, particularly in light of a continued adherence to the belief that the effect of Jewish schooling has a "delayed reaction," this study indicates that Jewish schooling has a positive immediate effect on its students' Jewish identification.

Certainly there were obvious exceptions to this suggestion. One mother had the impression that the immediate effect of Shalom School was negative. She said:

> I think it's incredible the kids come out not feeling bad about their Judaism.

A seventh grade student noted that both she and her Jewish friends who did not attend any Jewish school held similarly negative feelings towards being Jewish. She stated:

> They don't feel good about being Jewish, but I don't feel good about being Jewish and I go to Hebrew school.

Also, a few other students indicated as one boy did that he "hopes to be less Jewish as he grows older." However, the overwhelming amount of evidence indicated that the majority of students of Shalom School, regardless of their behavior in class, were identifying as Jews, were often feeling proud of being Jewish, and were being influenced by their experience at the school.

Survival and Identification

The type of identity and identification that the students developed closely reflected the type of identity and identification of their teachers and parents. The key element of their identity was understanding the element of being separate and apart from non-Jews. Their identification was built largely on anti-anti-semitic feelings coming, in part, from an on-going historical perspective that saw life only from the point of view of the Jew as an oppressed people, and which was unbending in its exclusion of all other perspectives. There was also a sense of pride in the Jewish people's ability to survive, in the nation of Israel, and in the tradition of pride in unspecified "traditions." There was no indication of there being anything more substantive in the students' Jewish identity than the "non-non-Jewish" understanding. There was, however, as indicated in Chapter Seven, considerable confusion and ambiguity regarding areas of values, concepts, and ideals that were sometimes attributed to the Jewish people.

Students, with their parents in agreement, recognized a difference between themselves and their Jewish friends who didn't attend any Jewish school. Also, they saw the difference as a result of the students' experience at the school rather than as a result of self-selection according to those who valued the school enough to attend and those who didn't. In this regard, one parent expressed a popular assessment about the most basic effect of the school:

> It is better than nothing. If you compare it to nothing then it is achieving its goals.

Speaking of the experience of her own daughter, she added:

> Two years ago before my daughter went, she didn't know she was Jewish. Well, she knew but she didn't know how to explain it. Now she knows how to explain it and she's very proud of it.

The feeling of pride as being a product of Shalom School training was echoed by an otherwise highly critical parent, who said:

They're getting something. It may be very little but it's better than nothing. They feel proud of being Jewish.

It was repeated over and over again that the school provided many of the children with their original source of identification as Jews. One former elementary student said:

> If there wasn't Hebrew School, most of these kids wouldn't even know they were Jewish.

Certainly many of the teachers agreed wholeheartedly that the school was providing the sole Jewish tie for a good many of their students. Said one teacher:

> If they didn't go to Hebrew school, what would they have? They know when holidays are because the school celebrates them.

Finally, many of the students mentioned that they were aware of a difference in attitude, knowledge, and particularly identification between themselves and their Jewish friends not attending any Jewish school. A comment of one girl was typical of many others:

> My other friend doesn't really go to Hebrew school. She's just Jewish. She doesn't really know anything.

One student even described some antagonism from Jewish friends who did not go to any Jewish school.

> They're not against me. But other Jewish people think I'm crazy because they don't go to Hebrew school.

On another level students and parents made comments giving an indication that the students' identification as Jews was in some small way taking a place in their lives, often in a positive sense, because of their pride in being Jewish. One mother described with some surprise the day her son came home from Shalom School checking to see if there was a Mezuzah[12] in the house because he suddenly believed that there should be one. A different student, who sounded very much like many of the parents of Shalom School students, described one way in which she demonstrated her tie with the Jewish people:

> It's something I am all the time, but I don't think about it all the time. If there is something on the radio about Israel or Jewish, I perk up.

A third student shocked her parents when she wore to school a pin her grandmother had sent that had a Jewish symbol on it. The significance of her action to her parent's way of thinking was made clear in their comments, as follows:

> Mother: Nomi received from her grandmother a pin with a Jewish star and American flag, and the last few days she's wearing it. I was really surprised and pleased.

Success in the Short-Term: Survival and Identification

Father: I was pleased, but I would never wear something like that—displaying my Jewishness!

Not only did some of the students display their Jewishness with various symbols, but a sizeable number of them reported that they actively asserted their Jewishness in public settings and among non-Jewish friends. One of the simplest ways some of the students openly interacted as Jews was to share their limited knowledge of Hebrew with classmates at public school. One fifth grade boy joked during class at Shalom School about how he spent the day at public school asking his friends in Hebrew whether they were a boy or girl. Another student explained that he and a Chinese friend taught one another simple words and phrases from each other's language:

Sometimes I speak Hebrew at school. I teach my friends Hebrew and my Chinese friend teaches me Chinese.

Still another student mentioned that friends would question her with interest when she would periodically speak to herself out loud in Hebrew.

Several students discussed with the researcher how they were made to feel uncomfortable at times in public school because they were Jewish. The reaction of some students was to be vocal and confront the source of their bad feelings. However, even among those who were more passive in their reaction, their pride in identifying and being identified as a Jew was not diminished and often strengthened. It seemed, too, that they found having the support of Jewish friends at Shalom School and just being a part of a Jewish school, offered them the extra strength needed to help them deal with those situations. Probably the most difficult time of the year for the Jewish students in this respect was the season during which Hanukah and Christmas fell. One student said:

We have Christmas parties in school and there's nothing else to do so I just do it. I don't like that.

Another student indicated to the researcher that he experienced problems around the time of most Jewish holidays, seemingly because it emphasized his different identification in being Jewish. He said:

Non-Jewish kids think it's weird [to be Jewish]. They tease us about it, but I just ignore it.

In another case, one student described the difficult circumstances encountered at home in identifying as a Jew. This boy's mother was Jewish and his father was Christian, and his father insisted on celebrating both Christmas and Hanukah in the household. The student said:

If we don't celebrate Christmas, he gets hot under the collar. But I feel funny on Christmas because it's not really my holiday.

Some of the students who reacted in a more active and verbal way to uncomfortable situations as Jews, reported that during holiday times they would explain to their public school classes about the Jewish holidays. One parent reported that her eleven-year-old son openly argued with his teacher about comments on Israel and other Jewish concerns and would sometimes challenge and correct the teacher's facts and information. Another student, a sixth grader whose friends knew he was Jewish but didn't really understand what that implied, described how he handled a potentially uncomfortable situation. The following conversation began when his non-Jewish friends came by his house just as he was leaving for Shalom School:

> They said, 'Hey, Louie. Where are you going?' And I told them I was going to catechism because I didn't want to go through the whole thing and explain it. And then I got home and explained the whole thing.

Finally, other children indicated their acceptance of the Jewish concern for Jewish survival and their fear and hatred of anti-semitism. In talking about his pride for Israel, one student explained:

> Israel is important. If the Nazis start up in America, then there is somewhere I can go.

Another student demonstrated her sensitivity to the issue of Jewish persecution in comparing her attitude with Jewish students who did not attend any Jewish school.

> Hanna: When we talk about Heil Hitler in school, they say yeah for him and I say boo for him.
> Researcher: You mean the Jewish kids?
> Hanna: Yeah. They know about him, but they say yeah and I say, boo. I don't like him!

It would be difficult, if not impossible, in a qualitative study to precisely sort out all the variables affecting Jewish identification. Certainly it seemed that both the influence of the home environment and the school could be important factors in affecting Jewish identification, at least in an immediate sense. Many of these home and school factors, furthermore, seemed to be interrelated. Not only did the school have an effect on its students, but it appeared as well to affect the parents, the home environment, and the synagogue, all of which, in turn, influenced the students, too. People associated with the school, however, did not recognize in any manner the important effect of the school in spheres beyond student concerns. While student identification as Jews was an important concern and effect of the school, the other factors may have been even more significant in terms of the long-reaching survival and structural concerns of the Jewish people. Of course, it was an initial parental decision that first established the school-child-family relationship. Those parents who were more certain of their identification as Jews, regardless of their Jewish school association, perhaps had already developed some strong sense of identification in their children. However, the school, through its attendance requirements and its inherent social nature, also allowed the children of this group of parents to establish their own independent ties to Jewish life and Jewish peer groups, and reinforced at least some of what was transmitted in the home.

The question of Jewish survival seemed closely linked, at least in some respects, to the Jewish people's identification as Jews. While the achievement of any sense of Jewish authenticity seemed unrealizable, and the comprehension of the substance of Jewish identity seemed much too enigmatic, the Jewish students did learn to see themselves as being apart and separate from the majority of the country, to be proud of their separateness, and to be on the alert to verbal, physical, or nonsensical attacks on themselves because they were Jewish. The Jewish students, while still thinking and acting just like all other students their age, came to appreciate the significance and permanence of their membership in this different "tribe." Many parents, too, while unchanged in almost all respects, either for the first time or in a sense of renewed understanding through their association with the school, realized the impact of their being a part of the Jewish group and rededicated themselves to that identification. Finally, the synagogue, a central force and gathering point for Jews in America, maintained its economic feasibility through its relationship with the school, and was able to continue on its own to attempt to retain its centrality and perpetuate Jewish life in America.

PART IV
ETHNIC SURVIVAL AND ETHNIC AUTHENTICITY

Chapter Ten

BEYOND SURVIVAL: IS THERE HOPE FOR SUBSTANCE AND AUTHENTICITY

The Jews are surviving. Not only are they not in danger of disappearance from assimilation, but this study shows that they are unusually expert in passing on survival skills. In particular, the Jewish supplementary school is used highly effectively for that purpose. But the emphasis on survival and the attraction to American culture and values has left many Jews with not much more than a survival culture as Jews. The Jews of Shalom School had great difficulty teaching and thinking about themselves as Jews beyond survival, and signs of substance and authenticity in Jewish life were hard to find.

The qualitative data of this study help give deeper meaning to the work of those who have looked at this same problem from a quantitative perspective (Cohen 1988; Goldscheider 1986, 1984; Himmelfarb 1974; Bock, 1976). The struggle of assimilation versus transformation is probably better understood as survival versus authenticity. The Jews are not about to disappear as the assimilationists fear; in fact this study shows just how well survival is taught. On the other hand, this close, in-depth inspection of the Jewish community shows few signs of transformation either. Indeed, while the statistical indicators of Jewish life and Jewish schooling may seem vibrant from a structural perspective, the quality of the Jewish experience within those structures continues to resemble the negative labels given by previous generations of social scientists describing a lack of substance and authenticity (Sklare 1967; Rosenthal 1970; Sartre 1965; Gans 1956; Cahnman 1955).

Long on Survival

In this study, perhaps the most distinctive quality of the Jewish people as an ethnic group was their instinct for survival. What concerned the Jewish people far more than issues of authenticity, identity or community were issues of defense. Authenticity, identity and community problems gained in importance, it seemed, only when through their absence they were perceived as threats to survival. The various conceptions of a Jewish "Way of Life" at Shalom School, so much discussed here, were secondary to a more vital and predominant concept of "survival" as the Jewish "Way of Life." Whether in times of actual threats and persecution, or in perceived states of freedom, the Jewish people were on constant guard.

Wirth notes (1943) that this concern for survival is precisely why Jewish schools have been so important historically. He writes that "while it has been concerned with the transmission of knowledge and skills of a sort, it has been primarily designed to nurture a consciousness of a common past and a common destiny." The common past that Wirth alludes to is taught as a history of oppression and persecution. At Shalom School, the transmission of a non-non-Jewish identity attempts to force a degree of separation from the majority culture so as to insure that total assimilation into a "free" American society will not occur. Simultaneously, the constant effort to instill an anti-anti-semitic identification through the school is yet another form of defense against overt, subtle, and imagined threats to Jewish survival. Indeed, the students of Shalom School may remember few if any facts, but they do keep with them the pain and suffering their ancestors suffered as they become vigilant to prevent any reoccurrences.

To conjecture about the survival of the Jewish people is to some extent foolhardy. Nevertheless, the immediate conflict of the Jews of Shalom School did not seem to be cause for concern for survival. What the school, in fact, did best was to teach a defensive posture, a constant guardedness against threats to Jewish survival.

In addition, the Jews of Shalom School seemed to be aware that their identification as Jews was something the world would never let them forget, even if they should try. They cherished their integration into American society, but they remained cautious and guarded in their security as Jews. As the rabbi of Shalom Synagogue commented:

> Why be Jewish? Even if they [the members] don't know why they come, still, they are coming. It's a way of continuing yourself. Why not? What will I be if I don't be Jewish? And the Holocaust has taught us that we don't have a choice.

Short on Substance

It is neither the intent of this book, nor within its scope, to prescribe authentic Jewishness or to present any prescribed formula for it. But the Jews of Shalom School, who themselves marked the distinction between their own behavior and attitudes and what they thought of as the Jewish "Way of Life," clearly represented a group who had lost any sense of authenticity for their Jewishness. This was not a conflict or debate over theological or ideological differences regarding authenticity, rather what existed was a virtual absence of theology or ideology. Indeed, beyond their "identity of separation" from other people, i.e., their non-non-Jewish identity, the people of Shalom School had only vague, ambiguous notions of their Jewishness.

Interestingly, Memmi writes (1962) that while Jewish institutions are so successful in protecting the Jews, in so doing they also are part of the cause of the lack of continuing growth and enlightenment. Indeed, one of the Shalom School teachers expressed the same thought:

I don't think Judaism will die out. People are proud of survival. There will be lots of assimilation and shrinkage, but I don't think it will die out. I think that's why people join synagogues but have nothing to do with Judaism in their lives.

At Shalom School, any understanding of Jewish life was set in historical or textual context without any recognition of application or synthesis with modern times. This factor clearly helped to separate people's daily routines from any Jewish substance. Not sensing any relevance or meaning from the fact of their Jewishness for the routines of their lives, the people of Shalom School continued to pattern their lives according to the lifestyle of the majority culture within this modern, capitalist, technologically advanced society. To these Jews, Jewish life and Jewish schooling were boring, uninteresting, unprofitable, unrewarding, and out-of-date. In contrast, the material values of secular society held highly desirable rewards and the age of technology and information held great interest. This generation of Jews, in particular, had achieved the American "dream," the material rewards of American society were accessible to them, and their desire and energy were devoted to accumulating those rewards and achieving an appropriately high level of socio-economic status.

The Jews of Shalom School clearly did not resemble the Jews of the Jewish history books and Jewish history in-the-making did not have much room for them either. A feature in the Los Angeles Times, profiling the changing Jewish community of Los Angeles, described the new generation of Jews as follows (Scheer, 1978):

> In the San Fernando Valley, where the new generation of Jews is found, the dreams are different.
> In the noisy dusk of Encino...music, horns, frozen yogurt, stores...cars jam up against the freeway and spill over into the lot of the synagogue school as parents pick up their teenagers who dream of cars, girls, alcohol and money, and who also happen to be Jewish.
> The Valley Jews, 150,000 strong, also the important Jews because they are the ones with family, with young... These are the new Jews who want a drink, who worry about divorce, who lost their jobs when the B-1 was scuttled, whose children may be bused... They [their homes] are often dotted with Pinkerton security signs instead of the mezuzoth called for in Jewish law.

Harold Schulweis (1978) wisely cautions not to write off these "new" Jews as bad Jews. He writes:

> We are not dealing with bad Jews. We are dealing with different Jews—Jews who are so radically different from our traditional adversaries that we cannot confront them with traditional polemic. We are not confronting apostates or assimilationists who oppose us on religious or ideological grounds. We are dealing with people who have an entirely different agenda of priorities and needs from the curricula and agenda that we represent.

However, the Jews of Shalom School and Schulweis' Jews hardly represent "transformed" Jews; rather these are the modern Jews, the surviving Jews, the non-substantive and inauthentic Jews.

Authenticity and the Limits of Cultural Pluralism

The need to adapt to modern life raises the dilemma of cultural pluralism: Is there a point beyond which adaptation and integration results in undesired effects? The problems associated with the high degree of integration with non-Jews, either in neighborhoods, schools, workplaces, marketplaces, or social settings suggests that such a high degree of self-imposed integration may not be conducive to living an authentic Jewish "Way of Life." Traditionally valued ideals such as education and family may need to undergo institutional adaptations, but the value of those ideals, as they had been so totally realigned with popular American ideals in Apple River, suggests that there must be places where authentic Jewish living can be practiced on a daily basis, with some protection from total immersion in the majority culture.

As an ideal, cultural pluralism acknowledges the differences among ethnic groups and at the same time affords equal status to them. Berkson (1920) described the goal of cultural pluralism for Jews as "the desire of the Jews to maintain their identity and to live the life of Jews in the midst of the social conditions of a divergent environment." What is suggested from the study of this Jewish community, however, is that in 20th century America there may be a point of largely voluntary integration and adaptation beyond which cultural pluralism doesn't work very well. At that point, pluralism may merely signify an ethnic minority group's continued survival. That survival may still be evidenced by certain unique integrative characteristics within the dominant society, however, as in this study, those unique characteristics may be so detached from any authentic characterization of the ethnic group that in actuality that group may resemble the dominant group more closely than the ethnicity of the group whose name it still goes by. Furthermore, it suggests that cultural pluralism, as Berkson described it, simply may not be workable in suburbia for these American Jews, because the conditions of suburbia, while not threatening survival, necessarily push intergroup relations towards a point of assimilation.

The reality of the situation for most Jews in America is that America, not Israel, is their home and will continue to be their home. Within America, the Jews' social position in society is to remain as an integrated ethnic minority. And that is the social context in which the Jews of Shalom School needed to confront the problems of identity, community, and authenticity.

The model of integrated pluralism (Newman 1973; Jaramillo 1977) as practiced by the Jews of Shalom School seemed most difficult to achieve. What the Jews needed was a compelling articulation of Jewish substance and authenticity that spoke to their lives as modern, upper-middle class, integrated Americans. These Jews were not rejecting a meaningful Jewish "Way of Life;" rather, they only understood it as being historical or taking place in Israel. Regrettably, it was not clear in any sense, what meaning it could have for them as an autonomous ethnic minority in America even if that meant having to take a few steps back from the very high degree of integrated pluralism now practiced. That clear articulation, in a form and language understood easily by the masses of Jews in the context of modern American life, is what was desperately needed and what was so glaringly absent.

The Jewish School: Its Role in Survival and Authenticity

The Jewish school teaches young Jews lessons on Jewish survival and does this well. In fact, it was from the very fact of the school's existence that its students and their parents learned most about Jewish identification. Unfortunately, on closer inspection of the school, one learned that beyond survival and identification it was confusion, deception, ambivalence, and ambiguity that characterized the condition of the Jews within this culturally pluralistic setting.

If the school is to teach about Jewish authenticity and substance, then it needs more than what the existing organizational structure allows. Ultimately, what the Jewish school needs in order to teach more than survival is a re-building of the Jewish community itself so that the socio-cultural context of the school is meaningful and substantive. To this end, what the school might do is to re-conceptualize its purpose to become a dynamic, purposeful institution using the resources of the school to help rebuild the community. This redefined Jewish school would have as its goals not just the transmission of the existing culture and community, but the rebuilding of the culture and community, the changing and transforming of the culture and the community, and participation in the culture and community.

One of the primary reactions of the Shalom School in responding to the problems it reflected from the state of Jewish life as a whole was to retreat from those problems. It did this through self-deception on the part of the school staff and on the part of some parents by focusing on an ideal of Jewish life portrayed in past history and by transferring that image onto themselves and their students within the school context.

By attempting to be more than a true reflection, or in some cases a dishonest reflection of Jewish society at large, the Jewish school and Jewish educators gave themselves an easy and often valid excuse for many of the criticisms to which they were subjected. However, in only accepting the role of technician, given the circumstances of Jewish life today, their work only served to perpetuate and exacerbate a problematic situation and a "survival" way of life.

The Jewish educators at Shalom School could redefine their own roles in the school from information bankers and technicians to that of planners, theoreticians, and change agents. As such, they could openly struggle with other educators in the community and throughout the country and with their students to identify and clarify the substance of authentic Jewish living. Cohen writes (1964:37):

> Let our children see us wrestling honestly and openly before them with our own problems as Jews. Let them sense our determination to wrest from our age-old Jewish tradition the meaning and relevance it must have for us and for mankind.

Under such conditions there could be an open admission and discussion of the conflicts of being a minority in a culturally pluralistic society, rather than a misleading presumption that "committed" Jews, supposedly such as those who were on the staff of Shalom School, are confident of all the "answers" and do not face such conflicts. Within Shalom School itself, development of social relations among peers, through cooperative rather than competitive learning, which could bond students together in Jewish-based friendships through life would have been an exceedingly important accomplishment for both community and identity (Bock 1976; Sleeper 1973). In addition, an active sense of community and common destiny needed to be extended to the relationship between teachers and parents. Their conflict, which was founded more out of frustration than substance, could be resolved through direct confrontation with the issues. (Schoem 1979)

Direct intervention by the school into the Jewish community at large is another approach that might be used for community change. Shalom School had the human resources and bodies necessary to help rejuvenate decaying institutions and to establish new ones. Jewish centers and neighborhood centers, adult education, old age homes, bookmobiles, kosher restaurants, stores and synagogues and the family itself, were just a few of the targets possible. Shalom School, in conjunction with other schools (again using human resources but in this case with older students), could train students to assert themselves politically in Jewish agencies, federations, synagogues, etc. to effect change.

At the same time, Shalom School might integrate itself to a much greater extent with the external Jewish community to effect change. Community organizations and individuals could be invited to the school more regularly to speak, present, consult and participate. Likewise, the school could send its students out to these places and people as a kind of youth corps, serving Jewish community needs.

On a broader scope, schooling itself might be redefined to lessen the existing distinction and separation between school and community. If students were actively serving the Jewish community, or taking classes at other Jewish centers, or studying closely with an individual mentor, that is, if one could receive a Jewish education in forms outside a school's walls, then that education ought to be recognized as a valid education. Beyond just recognition, education as so described could be actively encouraged, and in a Jewish community that was increasingly becoming an authentically Jewish community, education as such for both children and adults would be far more meaningful than the current textbook familiarity with Jewish life.

Implicit in these changes of course, are curricular changes, changes in the perceived importance of Jewish education, educational design according to Jewish principles, and extension of education beyond Bar/Bat Mitzvah to all age groups.

The initiation of an open discussion of problematic issues, the re-structuring of Jewish schooling to reflect a different image of Jewish society, the school's direct intervention into various aspects of Jewish life outside the traditional domain of the school and the redefining of Jewish education to include more than the idea that "schooling" currently connotes are some of the means by which the possibility that change might occur would increase. Furthermore, if the school could create a dynamic in which the Jewish community outside of the school was actively engaged in confronting the issues of identity and community dissolution in the integrated American setting, at that point it would be more likely that the school would witness meaningful change simply as a reflection of the substantively transformed Jewish community.

Comparative Perspectives and Future Research

While the history, experience, and current status of each group in the U.S. is obviously unique, a comparative study of the Jews in America with other American ethnic minority groups and their schools would be highly instructive. The Jewish community in America, because of its largely Ashkenazic[13] presence here has not had to face the inestimable problems of racism associated with skin color that have plagued non-white minorities in the United States in their attempts to achieve equal status with the white majority. The Jewish people, too, differ from other ethnic minorities in the U.S. in their current ability to maintain a relatively high socio-economic status. Nevertheless, one would expect to find all ethnic minority groups, regardless of color or socio-economic status, to be confronting at least some of the same categories of issues.

This researcher, in the context of this study, was able to briefly visit and meet with the directors of educational programs of two other ethnic minority groups located in Apple River. Furthermore, both groups seemed to be facing problems of identification as well as identity and seemed even less organized to face those issues than was the Jewish community.

The American Indian Center was associated with the local school district in Apple River although its services were available to people in three adjoining suburban cities. It had four staff members, a parent advisory committee, a library, audio-visual materials, and offered classes, tutorials, counseling and field trips. Its funding came from a federal grant. What the program was lacking, despite an estimated eight hundred students who qualified (by blood quantum) as American Indians, were people willing to participate in the Center. The director explained that a great many of these suburban American Indians who lived fully integrated lives in the majority culture, neither felt pride nor wanted to be identified publicly as American Indians by being associated with the school program. There were other administrative problems, too, that inhibited attendance, such as transportation to and from the Center after school. The director's new educational strategy, in response to his inability to attract more than a few handfuls of students to his center, was to pursue an active outreach program.

The other ethnic school in Apple River was organized by a local women's club and was coordinated by two volunteers. The three teachers and thirty-six students met one afternoon each week in a church school building. Although included in the school program was a cultural festival and the celebration of ethnic holidays, the program was otherwise strictly focused on language instruction. The primary concern of the school, as expressed by one of the coordinators, was to help their children identify with their ethnic background. She spoke matter-of-factly about the high rate of intermarriage and assimilation among the suburban ethnic population and stated that the younger children were not even aware that they were members of an ethnic group.

Just as there is a need for comparative ethnic minority studies in America, so, too, would qualitative comparative studies of Jewish communities and their schools be valuable. Jewish afternoon schools across America represent geographic regions, histories, finances, personalities, etc. that make each one different from the next. A comparative study of such schools and their communities would be very useful in assessing patterns of similarities and differences to the findings of this study of Shalom School and in developing a theory of Jewish schooling in America. One could assume that Shalom School was unique in many ways and faced different types of problems than other schools. Yet it is the impression of this researcher that a comparative study would find that the major categories of issues, conflicts, and dilemmas facing Shalom School were not very different from those present in Jewish schools across the nation. Problems in the areas of administration, physical location and structure, finances, distinctive personalities, etc. may have revealed themselves differently in different schools, but it is the opinion here that these types of issues are merely symptomatic of and external to the root cause of problems in the Jewish schools.

The researcher, in the context of this study, had the opportunity to briefly visit three other Jewish afternoon schools, two of which were affiliated with the "reform" movement, and one which was affiliated with the "orthodox" movement. Although these schools differed according to affiliation, the researcher's impression was that the problems of identity and community dissolution were still the major issues confronting the schools, and that with few exceptions the schools were acting self-deceptively and were not facing or attempting to resolve these problems. Furthermore, all of the schools were plagued to some degree by either building problems, finances, scheduling, difficult personalities, etc.

Finally, descriptions of schools and school problems in informal conversations with Jewish educators across the country, as well as in the literature on Jewish education cited herein also tend to confirm the gereralizability of Shalom School. It is the researcher's opinion that comparative studies will not find striking differences from the experience of Shalom School in the major categories of issues. Regardless of such future comparative findings, however, the case of Shalom School still stands on its own.

Finally, there is a need for comparative studies of Jewish communities within and outside the United States to study similarities and differences in the issues facing them and to study if and how other communities have proposed to confront and resolve those issues. There is also a valuable need for the Jewish people to compare their own experiences and dilemmas as an ethnic minority group in America with the experiences and dilemmas of other ethnic minorities. Studying the condition of Jews in other culturally pluralistic societies, and the experience of other ethnic minorities within America might allow for greater insight into the conflicts and dilemmas facing the Jews of America who are seeking to live authentically Jewish lives while remaining fully integrated in the majority culture.

It is the hope of this researcher that the insights from this study of Shalom School and the people associated with it will provide the stimulus for the Jewish people to actively seek out their authentic Jewish identity and rebuild their communal network. In so doing, perhaps the Jewish people will be able to speak of their Jewish identity in terms of substance and authenticity as well as in terms of survival, and they will again be able to find joy and fulfillment in their experience in Jewish education and in living the Jewish "Way of Life."

Notes

1. Six Million refers to the number of Jews killed in Nazi holocaust.
2. Bar/Bat Mitzvah refers to the ritual ceremony, held in a synagogue, in which a thirteen year old boy or girl reaches the status and assumes the duties of a Jewish "man" or "woman."
3. Bench Licht is a Yiddish expression meaning to recite the blessing over Sabbath or holiday candles.
4. "Joined" families refers to two single-parent families that are joined by marriage.
5. Tzedakah is a Hebrew word whose meaning includes righteousness, giving, charity.
6. A Siddur is a prayerbook.
7. Torah is the Five Books of Moses, from the Old Testament.
8. Tu Bishvat is the holiday celebrating the New Year for trees, the Jewish Arbor Day.
9. A Shofar is a ram's horn that is blown during the season of the High Holidays, Rosh Hashanah and Yom Kippur.
10. Strict observance of Jewish law does not permit using electricity on the Sabbath.

BIBLIOGRAPHY

Aberle, David
    1961 Culture and Socialization. *In* Physical Anthropology. Francis L.K. Hsu. Illinois: Dorsey Press.

Ackerman, Walter.
    1978 The New Curricula: Some Observations. *In* Conservative Judaism, Vol. 32, No. 1, Fall.
    1977 Some Uses of Justification in Jewish Education. *In* Association for Jewish Studies Vol, 2.
    1969 Jewish Education – For What. *In* American Jewish Yearbook, Vol. 70.

Banks, James
    1977 Cultural Pluralism: Implications for Curricular Reform. *In* Pluralism in a Democratic Society. Tumin and Plotch. New York: Praeger.

Beals, Alan R.
    1970 Gopalpur, 1958-1960. *In* Being an Anthropologist. George Spindler. New York: Holt, Rinehart and Winston.

Becker, Howard and Geer, Blanche
    1957 Participant Observation and Interviewing: A Comparison. *In* Human Organization.

Berkson, Isaac
    1920 Theories of Americanization. Teachers College, Columbia University. New York.

Blumer, Herbert
    1969 Symbolic Interactionism. New Jersey: Prentice-Hall.

Bock, Geoffrey
    1977 Does Jewish Schooling Matter. *In* Jewish Education and Jewish Identity. New York: American Jewish Committee.
    1976 The Social Context of Jewish Education: A Literature Review. *In* Jewish Education and Jewish Identity. New York: American Jewish Committee.
    1976 The Jewish Schooling of American Jews: A Study of Non-cognitive Educational Effects. Unpublished Doctoral Dissertation. Harvard University.

Boissevain, Jeremy
    1970 Fieldwork in Malta. *In* Being An Anthropologist. George Spindler. New York: Holt, Rinehart and Winston.

Brody, Arthur
 1978 Workshop on Planning and Financing Jewish Education. Advance Report for Community Discussion. Council of Jewish Federations, Nov. 9 (Xerox).

Bronfenbrenner, Urie
 1973 Two Worlds of Childhood: U.S. and USSR. New York: Pocket Books.

Byrne, Susan
 1974 Arden, An Adult Community. *In* Anthropologists in Cities. George Foster and Robert Kemper, Boston: Little, Brown and Co.

Cahnman, Werner
 1955 Suspended Alienation and Apathetic Identification. Jewish Social Studies, 17, July.

Carmichael, Stokely and Charles Hamilton
 1967 Black Power: The Politics of Liberation in America. New York: Vintage Books.

Carnoy, Martin
 1974 Education as Cultural Imperialism. New York: David McKay Co.

Cassell, Joan
 1978 A Fieldwork Manual for Studying Desegregated Schools. Washington, D.C.: National Institute of Education, HEW.

Castaneda, Alfredo.
 1974 Persisting Ideological Issues of Assimilation in America. *In* Cultural Pluralism. Edgar Epps. Berkeley: McCutchan Pub.

Castaneda, Alfredo, Richard James and Webster Robbins
 1974 The Educational Needs of Minority Groups. Professional Educators Publications.

Cohen, Jack
 1964 Jewish Education in a Democratic Society. New York: Reconstructionist Press.

Cohen, Steven M.
 1988 American Assimilation or Jewish Revival. Bloomington: Indiana University.
 1987 The One in 2000 Controversy. *In* Moment. March.
 1983 American Modernity and Jewish Identity. New York: Tavistock Publications.
 1974 The Impact of Jewish Education on Religious Identification and Practice. *In* Jewish Social Studies. 36, July-Oct.

Dashefsky, Arnold
 1972 And the Search Goes On: The Meaning of Religio-Ethnic Identity and Identification. *In* Sociological Analysis, Vol. 33, No. 4, Winter.

Dashefsky, Arnold and Howard Shapiro
 1974 Ethnic Identification Among American Jews. Mass.: D.C. Heath and Co.

Bibliography

Dean, John P., Robert Eichhorn and Lois Dean
    1962 Limitations and Disadvantages of Unstructured Methods. *In* American Journal of Sociology, 67.

DeVos, George
    1975 Ethnic Pluralism: Conflict and Accommodation. *In* Ethnic Identity. George DeVos and Lola Romanucci-Ross, eds. Palo Alto: Mayfield Pub.

Dreeben, Robert
    1968 On What is Learned in School. Reading, Mass.: Addison-Wesley.

Dushkin, Alexander
    1966 Aims of Jewish Education in the Diaspora. *In* Judaism and the Jewish School. Judah Pilch, New York: Bloch Publishing.
    1918 Jewish Education in New York City. New York Bureau of Jewish Education.

Dushkin, Alexander and Uriah Z. Engelman
    1959 Jewish Education in the United States. New York: American Association for Jewish Education.

Elazar, Daniel
    1973 Decision-making in the Jewish Community. *In* The Future of the Jewish Community. David Sidorsky, ed. New York: Basic Books.

Epps, Edgar, ed.
    1974 Cultural Pluralism. Berkeley: McCutchan Publishing.

Epstein, Noel
    1977 Language, Ethnicity and the Schools. George Washington University: Institute for Educational Leadership. Washington, D.C.

Everhart, Robert
    1976 Ethnography and Educational Policy: Love and Marriage or Strange Bedfellows. *In* CAE Quarterly, Vol. 7, No. 3, August.

Fox, Seymour
    1977 Toward a Philosophy of Jewish Education. *In* Jewish Education and Jewish Identity. New York: American Jewish Committee, 1977.
    1973 Toward A General Theory of Jewish Education. *In* The Future of the Jewish Community. David Sidorsky, ed. New York: Basic Books.

Friedman, Ahuva
    1979 Memorandum Re: Size of United Synagogue Congregations. United Synagogue of America, April 25.

Gallimore, Ronald, Boggs Joan Whitehorn and Cathie Jordan
    1974 Culture, Behavior, and Education: A Study of Hawaiian-Americans. Beverly Hills, Ca.: Sage Publications.

Gamoran, Emanuel
    1925 Changing Conceptions in Jewish Education, Book Two. New York: The Macmillan Co.

Gannes, Abraham, ed.
  1965 Selected Writings of Leo H. Honor. Reconstructionist Press.
Gans, Herbert
  1956 American Jewry: Present and Future. *In* Commentary, Vol. 21, No. 5+6, May and June.
Gartner, Lloyd, ed.
  1969 Jewish Education in the U.S. New York: Teachers College Press.
Gearing, Fred
  1973 Where We Are and Where We Might Go: Steps Toward a General Theory of Cultural Transmission. *In* CAE Quarterly, Vol. 4, No. 1, Feb.
Glazer, Nathan
  1972 The Social Background of American Jewish Education. *In* Jewish Education and Jewish Identity. New York: American Jewish Committee.
  1954 Ethnic Groups in America: From National Culture to Ideology. *In* Freedom and Control in Modern Society. Monroe Berger, I. Abel, Charles Page. New York: D. Van Nostrand and Co.
Glazer, Nathan and Daniel Patrick Moynihan
  1963 Beyond the Melting Pot. Cambridge, Mass.: Harvard University Press.
Gold, Raymond
  1958 Roles in Sociological Field Observations. *In* Social Forces, 36.
Goldscheider, Calvin
  1986 The American Jewish Community. Atlanta: Scholars Press.
Goldscheider, Calvin and Alan S. Zuckerman
  1984 The Transformation of the Jews. Chicago: University of Chicago Press.
Goodlad, John L.
  1977 What Goes on in Our Schools? *In* Educational Researcher, Vol. 6, No. 3.
Gordon Milton
  1975 Towards a General Theory of Racial and Ethnic Group Relations. *In* Ethnicity. Nathan Glazer and Daniel Patrick Moynihan, eds. Cambridge, Mass.: Harvard University Press.
  1964 Assimilation in American Life. New York: Oxford University Press.
Grindal, Bruce
  1972 Growing Up in Two Worlds: Education and Transition Among the Sisala of Northern Ghana. San Francisco: Holt, Rinehart and Winston.
Heilman, Samuel
  1984 Inside the Jewish School. New York: American Jewish Committee.
Herberg, Will
  1953 Protestant-Catholic-Jew. New York: Doubleday and Co.

Herman, Simon
　1977 Jewish Identity, A Social Psychological Perspective. Beverly Hills, Ca.: Sage Publications.

Himmelfarb, Harold
　1978 Patterns of Assimilation – Identification Among American Jews. *In* Ethnicity.
　1976 Fertility Trends and Their Effects on Jewish Education. *In* Analysis.
　1975 Jewish Education for Naught – Educating the Culturally Deprived Child. *In* Analysis, No. 51.
　1974 The Impact of Religious Schooling: The Effects of Jewish Education Upon Adult Religious Involvement. Unpublished Ph.D. Dissertation, University of Chicago.

Hochberg, Hillel and Gerhard Lang
　1974 The Jewish High School in 72-73: Status and Trends. *In* American Jewish Yearbook, Vol. 75.

Hostetler, John and Gertrude E. Huntington
　1971 Amish Society, Socialization and Community Education. New York: Holt, Rinehart and Winston.

Isajiw, Wsevolod W.
　1974 Definitions of Ethnicity. *In* Ethnicity, 1, No. 2, July.

Jaramillo, Mari-Luci
　1977 Cultural Pluralism: Implications for Curriculum. *In* Pluralism in a Democratic Society. Melvin Tumin and Walter Plotch, eds. New York: Praeger Publishers.

Kallen, Horace
　1956 Cultural Pluralism and the American Idea. Philadelphia: University of Pennsylvania Press.
　1954 Of Them Which Say They Are Jews. Judah Pilch, ed. New York: Bloch Publishing.
　1932 Judaism at Bay: Essays Toward the Adjustment of Judaism to Modernity. New York: Bloch Publishing Co.
　1924 Culture and Democracy in the United States. New York: Boni and Liveright.

Kelman, Herbert
　1977 The Place of Jewish Identity in the Development of Personal Identity. *In* Jewish Education and Jewish Identity. American Jewish Committee.

Kessen, William, ed.
　1975 Childhood in China. New Haven: Yale University Press.

Khlief, Bud
　1974 Issues in Anthropological Fieldwork in the Schools. *In* Education and Cultural Processes. George Spindler, ed. New York: Holt, Rinehart and Winston.

King, Richard A.
  1967 The School at Mopass: A Problem of Identity. New York: Holt, Rinehart and Winston.

Krug, Mark
  1976 The Melting of the Ethnics. Indiana: Phi Delta Kappan.

Kurokawa, Minako, ed.
  1970 Minority Responses. New York: Random House.

LaBelle, Thomas
  1972 An Anthropological Framework for Studying Education. *In* Teachers College Record, Vol. 4, No. 4, May.

Landman, Isaac
  1939 Survival Values in Jewish Religious Education. *In* Religious Education, 34, July-Sept.

Lang, Gerhard
  1968 Jewish Education. *In* American Jewish Yearbook, Vol. 69.

Lavender, Abraham
  1975 Disadvantages of Minority Group Membership: The Perspective of a 'Nondeprived' Minority Group. *In* Ethnicity 2, No. 1, March.

Lazerwitz, Bernard
  1973 Religious Identification and Its Ethnic Correlates: A Multivariate Model. *In* Social Forces, 52, Winter.

Lewin, Kurt
  1970 Resolving Social Conflicts. *In* Minority Responses. Minako Kurokawa, ed. New York: Random House.

Lieber, David
  1978 Staking Out the Conservative Position. *In* Conservative Judaism, Vol. 32, No. 1, Fall.

Liebman, Charles
  1973 The Ambivalent American Jew. Philadelphia: Jewish Publication Society.

Lindesmith, A.R., and Strauss, A.L.
  1968 Social Psychology. New York: Holt, Rinehart and Winston.

Lipnick, Bernard
  1976 An Experiment That Works. New York: Bloch Publishing.

Lofland, John
  1971 Analyzing Social Settings. Belmont, Calif.: Wadsworth Pub.

Lutz, Frank W. and Margaret A. Ramsey
  1974 The Use of Anthropological Field Methods in Education. *In* Educational Researcher, 3 (10), Nov.

Macias, Reynaldo F., et al.
   1975 Educacion Alternativa: On the Development of Bilingual Chicano Schools. Hayward, Calif.: The Southwest Network.

Marcus, Lloyd
   1961 The Treatment of Minorities in Secondary School Textbooks. New York: ADL of Bnai Brith.

Maslow, Will
   1974 The Structure and Functioning of the American Jewish Community. New York: American Jewish Congress.

McCall, George J.
   1969 Data Quality Control in Participant-Observation. *In* Issues in Participant Observation. George McCall and J.L. Simmons, eds. Mass.: Addison-Wesley.

McLuhan, Marshall and Quentin Fiore
   1967 The Medium is the Massage. New York: Bantam Books.

Memmi, Albert
   1966 The Liberation of the Jew. New York: Viking Press.
   1962 Portrait of a Jew. New York: Viking Press.

Michaelis, John U.
   1972 Social Studies for Children in A Democracy: Recent Trends and Developments. Fifth Edition. Englewood Cliffs, Prentice-Hall.

Michaelis, John, Ruth Grossman and Lloyd Scott
   1975 New Designs for the Elementary School Curriculum. New York: McGraw-Hill.

Miller, S.M.
   1952 The Participant Observer and Over-Rapport. *In* American Sociological Review, 17.

Newman, William M.
   1973 American Pluralism. New York: Harper and Row.

Novak, Michael.
   1977 Cultural Pluralism for Individuals: A Social Vision. *In* Pluralism in a Democratic Society. Tumin and Plotch, eds. New York: Praeger.

Nyerere, Julius
   1968 Ujamaa, Essays on Socialism. London: Oxford University Press.

Ogbu, John
   1978 Minority Education and Caste: The American System in Cross-Cultural Perspective. New York: Academic Press.
   1974 The Next Generation: An Ethnography of Education in an Urban Neighborhood. New York: Academic Press.

Overholt, George and William Stallings
 1976 Ethnographic and Experimental Hypotheses in Educational Research. *In* Educational Researcher, Vol. 5, No. 8, Sept.

Parsons, Talcott
 1975 Some Theoretical Considerations on the Nature and Trends of Change of Ethnicity. *In* Ethnicity. Nathan Glazer and Daniel P. Moynihan, eds. Cambridge: Harvard University Press.
 1959 The School Class as a Social System: Some of its Functions in American Society. *In* Harvard Educational Review, Vol. 29, No. 4, Fall.

Pilch, Judah
 1977 Between Two Generations. New York: Bloch Publishing.
 1966 Judaism and the Jewish School. New York: Bloch Publishing.
 1963 Fate and Faith: The Contemporary Jewish Scene. New York: Bloch Publishing.

Rockowitz, Murray and Gerhard Lang
 1976 Trends in Jewish School Enrollment in the United States 1974/75. New York: American Association for Jewish Education.

Rosenthal, Erich
 1970 Acculturation Without Assimilation? The Jewish Community of Chicago, Ill. *In* Minority Responses. Minako Kurokawa, ed. New York: Random House.

Rosten, Leo
 1970 The Joys of Yiddish. New York: Pocket Books.

Sartre, Jean Paul
 1965 Antisemite and the Jew. New York: Shocken Books.

Schatzman, Leonard and Anselm Strauss.
 1973 Field Research. Strategies for a Natural Sociology. New Jersey: Prentice-Hall.

Scheer, Robert
 1978 L.A. Jews: New Set of Values for the Middle Class. *In* Los Angeles Times, Feb. 1.

Scheffler, Israel
 1971 How Can a Jewish Self-Consciousness Be Developed? *In* The Study of Jewish Identity: Issues and Approaches. S.N. Herman, ed. Jerusalem: Institute of Contemporary Jewry, Hebrew University.

Schermerhorn, R.A.
 1970 Comparative Ethnic Relations: A Framework for Theory and Research. New York: Random House.

Schoem, David
- 1988A Learning to be a Part-Time Jew. *In* Persistence and Flexibility: Anthropological Perspectives of the American Jewish Experience. Walter Zenner, ed. New York: SUNY Press.
- 1988B Mediating Ethnic Minority Conflict in the Classroom: The Case of Blacks and Jews. *In* Working Papers. Ann Arbor: Program in Conflict Management Alternatives (University of Michigan).
- 1984A Jewish Schooling and Jewish Survival in the Suburban American Community. *In* Studies in Jewish Education, Vol. 2. Michael Rosenak, ed. Jerusalem: Magnes Press, Hebrew University.
- 1984B Improving School Climate in an Afternoon School. *In* Pedagogic Reporter, Vol. 35, No. 4, October.
- 1983A Seeing is Disbelieving: Researching Curriculum Through Ethnography. *In* Studies in Jewish Education, Vol. 1. Barry Chazan, ed. Jerusalem: Magnes Press, Hebrew University
- 1983B What the Afternoon School Does Best. *In* Jewish Education, Vol. 51, No. 54, Winter.
- 1982 Explaining Jewish Student Failure and Its Implications. *In* Anthropology and Education Quarterly, Vol. 13, No. 4, Winter.
- 1981A Uncovering the Classroom Through Anthropological Analysis. New York: American Jewish Committee.
- 1981B Going to Hebrew School Won't Get You Into Harvard. *In* Genesis II, May.
- 1980 Inside the Classroom: Reflections of a Troubled People. *In* Jewish Education, Vol. 48, No. 1, Spring.
- 1979 The Parent as Scapegoat in Jewish Education. *In* A Sampler of Jewish Educational Thought and Teaching. Sheldon Dorph, ed. Los Angeles: CAJE.
- 1977 Approaches to Jewish Education: A Modern Guide for Principals, Teachers, and Students. Unpublished manuscript.

Schulweis, Harold M.
- 1978 The Public and Private Agenda in Jewish Education. *In* The Pedagogic Reporter, Vol. 30, No. 1, Fall.

Shapiro, Howard and Arnold Dashefsky
- 1974 Religious Education and Ethnic Identification: Implications for Ethnic Pluralism. *In* Review of Religious Research, Vol. 15, No. 2, Winter.

Sidorsky, David
- 1976 Summary Report and Recommendations: Colloquium on Jewish Education and Jewish Identity. *In* Jewish Education and Jewish Identity. New York: American Jewish Committee.

Sidorsky, David, ed.
- 1973 The Future of the Jewish Community. New York: Basic Books.

Siegel, Richard, Michael Strassfeld and Sharon Strassfeld
   1973 The Jewish Catalogue. Philadelphia: Jewish Publication Society.
Silberman, Charles
   1985 A Certain People: American Jews and Their Lives Today. New York: Summit.
   1977 Goals and Practice in Jewish Education: A Personal Perspective. *In* Jewish Education and Jewish Identity. New York: American Jewish Committee.
   1976 Where Are Our Children. *In* Moment, Vol. 1, No. 6, Jan.
Sklare, Marshall
   1971 America's Jews. New York: Random House.
Sklare, Marshall and Greenblum, Jr.
   1967 Jewish Identity on the Suburban Frontier. New York: Basic Books.
Sleeper, James
   1973 A Radical View of Jewish Culture. *In* The Future of the Jewish Community. David Sidorsky, ed. New York: Basic Books.
Sowell, Thomas
   1981 Ethnic America. New York: Basic Books.
Spindler, George
   1976 From Omnibus to Linkages: Cultural Transmission Models. *In* Educational Patterns and Cultural Configurations. Joan Roberts and Sherrie Akinsanya, eds. New York: Holt, Rinehart and Winston.
   1974 The Transmission of Culture. *In* Education and Cultural Processes. George Spindler, ed. New York: Holt, Rinehart, and Winston.
Spindler, George, ed.
   1970 Being an Anthropologist: Fieldwork in Eleven Cultures. New York: Holt, Rinehart, and Winston.
Spindler, George and Louise Spindler
   ____ Foreword. *In* Case Studies in Education and Culture. New York: Holt, Rinehart, and Winston.
Steinberg, Steven
   1981 The Ethnic Myth. Boston: Beacon Press.
Stone, Gerald and Neil Newman
   1975 Investigation of Goals in a Jewish Congregational School. *In* Jewish Education, Vol. 43, No. 4, Winter-Spring.
Stone, G.P.
   1962 Appearance and the Self. *In* Human Behavior and Social Processes. A.M. Rose, ed. Boston: Houghton Mifflin.
Strauss, Anselm, et al.
   1969 Field Tactics. *In* Issues in Participant Observation. McCall and Simmons, eds. Mass.: Addison-Wesley.

Tumin, Melvin and Walter Plotch, eds.
  1977 Pluralism in a Democratic Society. New York: Praeger Publishers.

Vidich, Arthur and Gilbert Shapiro
  1955 A Comparison of Participant Observation and Survey Data. *In* American Sociological Review, Vol. 20.

Waller, Willard
  1932 The Sociology of Teaching. New York: J. Wiley and Sons.

Warner, W. Lloyd and William Srole
  1945 The Social Systems of American Ethnic Groups. New Haven: Yale University Press (Yankee City Series, Vol. 3).

Waxman, Chaim
  1983 America's Jews in Transition. Philadelphia: Temple University Press.

Waxman, Mordecai
  1976 Surviving the Infertile Years: The Synagogue and the Community. *In* Analysis.

Weinberger, Paul
  1971 The Effects of Jewish Education. *In* American Jewish Yearbook, Vol. 72.

Winter, Nathan
  1966 Jewish Education in a Pluralist Society: Samson Benderly and Jewish Education in the United States. New York: New York University Press.

Wirth, Louis
  1943 Education for Survival: The Jews. *In* American Journal of Sociology, 48:6, May.

Wolcott, Harry
  1973 The Man in the Principal's Office: An Ethnography. New York: Holt, Rinehart, and Winston.

Wolfson, Ronald G.
  1974 A Description and Analysis of an Innovative Living Experience in Israel. Unpublished Doctoral Dissertation, Washington University (St. Louis).

Zelditch, Morris, Jr.
  1962 Some Methodological Problems of Field Studies. *In* American Journal of Sociology.

www.ingramcontent.com/pod-product-compliance
Lightning Source LLC
Chambersburg PA
CBHW021127300426
44113CB00006B/322